P9-DFS-314

## HOW DOES A DAUGHTER SURVIVE
## THE LOSS OF A MOTHER'S LOVE?

"More than a decade after my mother's death, I still converse with her."

"As my mother told me one day before she went into the hospital for the first time, 'You may not always hear me, but you'll always feel my answer.'"

"I'd learned to express my love for her whenever I felt it. I didn't need to see my mother's body for closure. . . . I chose instead to live with the memories of my mother full of life, and not without it."

"The closer I get to her age [at death], the clearer it becomes to me that we each were given our own paths to walk in life. Believing in this gives me huge amounts of freedom and joy."

OTHER BOOKS BY HOPE EDELMAN

*Motherless Daughters*

# LETTERS FROM

# Motherless
# Daughters

### WORDS OF COURAGE, GRIEF, AND HEALING

EDITED AND WITH AN INTRODUCTION BY

## HOPE EDELMAN

Delta
Trade Paperbacks

A Delta Book
Published by
Dell Publishing
a division of
Bantam Doubleday Dell Publishing Group, Inc.
1540 Broadway
New York, New York 10036

Many of the designations used by manufacturers and sellers to distinguish their products are claimed as trademarks. Where those designations appear in this book and Addison-Wesley was aware of a trademark claim, the designations have been printed in initial capital letters (i.e., Tylenol).

Motherless Daughters is a trademark and service mark of Hope Edelman, for use with instructional and teaching materials, support groups, seminars, workshops, and other related activities.

Copyright © 1995 by Hope Edelman

All rights reserved. No part of this book may be reproduced or transmitted in any form or by any means, electronic or mechanical, including photocopying, recording, or by any information storage and retrieval system, without the written permission of the Publisher, except where permitted by law. For information address Addison-Wesley Publishing Company, Reading, Massachusetts.

The trademark Delta® is registered in the U.S. Patent and Trademark Office and in other countries.

ISBN: 0-385-31522-8

Reprinted by arrangement with Addison-Wesley Publishing Company

Manufactured in the United States of America
Published simultaneously in Canada

May 1996

10 9 8 7 6

BVG

FOR MY AUNT ROSALIE,
WHO IS DEEPLY MISSED

# CONTENTS

# ACKNOWLEDGMENTS

To Elizabeth Kaplan, my agent, for her tireless work on my behalf; Nancy Miller, my editor, for her enthusiasm and remarkable speed; Gail Eisenberg, for her superb assistance in all matters editorial, organizational, and postal; Judith Hirsch, for tea and calculations; Joe Bargmann, at *Seventeen*, for his help from the very start; Leslie Schnur and Jackie Cantor, at Dell, for being in on the brainstorm; Diane Hambrook, for giving so freely of herself; Jonathan, Amy, Sharon, and Ty, for keeping me out on the streets; Debbie, Eve, Jane, Julie, Lauren, Raya, and Naomi, for validating everything; and Phil and Kitty, for giving me a warm and loving second home: Thanks.

# PREFACE

In the letters and phone calls I received after the
publication of *Motherless Daughters*, many of the
women who'd read the book asked for more. They
wanted more stories from other women who'd lost
their mothers, more information about the grieving
process, and further assurance that their experience
was not a unique or isolated one. Hundreds of
women sent me their personal stories of mother loss,
and many of them generously volunteered to partici-
pate in a subsequent book.

Letters from Motherless Daughters has been com-
piled to fulfill these requests. The fifty-eight women
whose letters appear in this book come from twenty-
four states in the United States and three provinces
in Canada. They range in age from thirteen to seventy-eight, with an average age of thirty-five. The
majority of these women wrote to me after reading

*Motherless Daughters*. Others wrote in response to the initial ads I'd placed when looking for motherless women to interview, and after reading articles I'd written for *Special Report*, the *San Francisco Chronicle*, the *St. Paul Pioneer Press*, and *Seventeen*. The letters have been edited for reasons of space, but I have retained their original language and syntax as often as possible. In exchange for the use of these letters, I have promised anonymity to their writers. All of the names that appear in this book are pseudonyms.

# INTRODUCTION

After fourteen years without a mother, I am no stranger to searching. I can lose myself in an atlas for hours, and by now I've called five different cities home. So in 1992 and 1993, when I was writing *Motherless Daughters*, it felt oddly appropriate to spend hours in libraries and bookstores searching for books about grief. Those afternoons reminded me of the solitary library sojourns I used to make in college, looking for information about the long-term effects of early mother loss. Back then, my family wasn't talking about my mother's death from breast cancer at age forty-two, and I didn't know anyone in my peer group whose mother had died. A book seemed to be a safe and private way to check my feelings against some sort of standard, and I hoped to find one that would help explain what I was feeling—why, in spite of all my valiant attempts at stoicism, I still missed my mother ten months, two years, and then four years after she had died.

In 1982, my efforts were premature. Despite the plethora of books written about mother-daughter relationships, I found virtually nothing for a woman who'd lost her mother at an early age. Ten years later I was slightly more successful in my quest. Grief had become a fertile ground for writers in the 1980s, and I found self-help books about coping after the loss of a loved one; academic texts about the mourning process in general; psychology books about losing a parent specifically; and first-person narratives by sons and daughters who told their stories of loss, pain, and recovery.

Still, the library shelves didn't address my specific need. Most of these "grief" texts emphasized crisis management over long-term adaptation, failing to acknowledge that part of the adjustment process after the death of a loved one includes maintaining a relationship—albeit a new relationship—with that person. The books I found accurately described the emotional roller coaster we all ride for the first six or eight months after the death of a loved one, but they didn't explain how we should, or could, be feeling five or ten or twenty years after the loss.

I suppose there's a logical reason for this: who, after all, wants to read a book immediately after losing a mother and learn that the mourning process is likely to continue for several decades? We'd all like to believe that mourning is magically contained within those first six months after a loss. I felt lousy enough when my mother died in 1981. I didn't want to hear that I'd still miss her in another ten years.

People in pain naturally search for a quick fix, and I admit that until only recently I was no exception. When I began writing *Motherless Daughters*, I hoped the two years I planned to devote to the book would provide me with an intense, self-contained period of grief that I could eventually exit and finally (finally, finally, finally) feel that I didn't long for my mother—or *a* mother—anymore.

But once I began speaking with and receiving letters from other motherless women, I began to realize how unrealistic my expectation was. Instead of meeting women who revealed their personal prescriptions for a mourning cure, I found myself collecting stories from daughters who, as many as thirty years after their mothers' deaths, continued to renegotiate their relationships with their mothers and admitted to missing their mothers (and, yes, crying for them) still.

At first, I found this profoundly discouraging. "How can I write a book telling women that mourning for a mother never really ends?" I remember asking a friend. "That's not a very hopeful message."

Granted, it's not overly optimistic, but it does happen to be true. A daughter's mourning for a lost mother never completely stops. Instead, it evolves over time, often leading a woman to a place where, instead of actively grieving, she can describe the feeling as a sense of "missing" her mother, and where she can even begin to see some long-term positive outcomes of early mother loss.

This theory of ongoing mourning is hardly revolutionary. A few psychologists—often those who suffered a dramatic, early loss themselves—have been aware of this process for years. In her recent book *No Voice Is Ever Wholly Lost*, Louise J. Kaplan explains why the linear model of grief (acknowledgment, detachment, and return to reality) shortchanges and ultimately fails those of us who've lost a loved one:

> The process of mourning is not only about detachment and the gradual relinquishment of the lost one, it is also about a reconfirmation of our attachments. The *full* work of mourning encompasses the rebuilding of our inner world and the restoration of the beloved in the form of an inner presence—if not precisely a Spirit or a ghost, an aspect of ego or conscience, an ideal, a passion. Over the course of time, these inner presences may undergo further development and revision, but they will never leave us. We can call on our inner presences to join us in the morning over coffee and rolls, to help us fold the laun-

dry properly, to guide us in planting a garden, to inspire a painting, to give us the courage to protest social injustice.

Long after the return of logic and reason, long after we rejoin the world of the living, we are still attached to our lost ones. The human dialogue—that which makes living a life worthwhile—goes on. In the absence of this dialogue, we are lost.

More than a decade after my mother's death, I still converse with her. Constantly. I consult her for insights about my father, we argue about getting married, and she urges me to play the piano again. For years this dialogue was my secret, the glaring evidence, I was certain, of a daughter whose mourning had gone awry. The discovery that I was not a mutant griever but was, in fact, quite normal for a daughter who'd lost her mother was a moment of pure liberation and relief. For the first time, I felt I didn't have to hide the pain of mother loss; I could accept it as a part of my past and present and get on with enjoying my life. As Sheryl, a thirty-seven-year-old woman who was fourteen when her mother died in an auto accident, writes:

> I've missed my mother so much throughout my life stages—my graduations, my wedding, the births of my two daughters—that I

was surprised by the hurt I feel now. I woke up on my thirty-seventh birthday this year crying, because when my mother was thirty-seven she had only one more year to live and she didn't even know it.

I realized I needed some help to get through this, and I'm finally in therapy. (Something I have wanted to do for a while, but the time or money never seemed to be available.) I wasn't prepared for the depth of my pain, though. When you cover a wound like this and try to live, you forget that the wound goes to the very core of your being. Death is something we're supposed to "get over" in this society. It is so good and healing to hear my therapist say what is true: I'll never "get over" the death of my mother. It is a stone that will always weigh heavy in my heart. I like to think of therapy as the process of turning that stone from dense, heavy granite to a light, porous pumice. The stone will never be beautiful or smooth to the touch. But I can use that pumice to grind down the rough edges of my life. I can learn to live with this loss.

Sheryl's ability to reframe her loss as a past event that she can use today allows her to attach meaning to the loss and see it as a transformational experience. All losses are transformational, whether we're able to accept them as such or not. The self that existed before a major life event is not quite the same self that walks away from that event. As the author Diane Cole, who was twenty-two when her mother died of cancer, writes in her memoir, *After Great Pain*, "In the aftermath of any loss, we begin to reexamine and redefine ourselves, our values, and our possibilities, until a new life emerges."

Daughters who lose their mothers at a very young age usually aren't aware of the transformational quality of the loss when it occurs; its impact may not become evident for years. Over time, however, most of us grow to acknowledge a mother's death as a clear point of demarcation in our lives. The novelist and columnist Anna Quindlen, who was nineteen when she lost her mother to cancer, has described the event as "the dividing line between the self I am and the self I became." Thirty-four-year-old Caitlin, who also was nineteen when her mother died, describes an even more dramatic watershed: "I feel that my life is kind of divided into 'Mom' and 'post-Mom' sections," she explains. "The change started with her illness, but on the day of her death life shifted for me."

One of our biggest challenges as adult daughters without mothers is to find a way to see our losses as points of departure rather than as a set of lead weights. In this book, you will read the words of motherless women who, over the years, have discovered how to use their loss as a catalyst for change, and who are trying to embrace and accept that change today. You will also hear the stories of women still struggling to accept and understand the profound losses they have experienced. In their own words, they describe their mourning processes and the lingering effects of early mother loss: how it can continue to replay itself through later losses; inspire a fear of subsequent loss; lead a daughter to idealize a less-than-perfect mother; affect long-term relationships with fathers, siblings, and other relatives; influence the decisions a woman makes about her job, home, and friends; and impact her role as a partner, wife, and mother.

Lise Funderberg, writing for *Mirabella* magazine, aptly described motherless women as an "unsought sorority." We may not have chosen to join this exclusive group, but once initiated we're bound by shared experience. The motherless women whose letters appear in this book clearly constitute a sisterhood. Even though the details of their stories of loss and adaptation vary greatly, similar thoughts and experiences reverberate throughout the book. While reading through the original stack of letters, I could hear my younger self speaking in the words of the teen-aged girls; locate myself now in the letters from adult women still struggling to understand and accommodate their early losses; and, from the stories of older women, imagine how I might still be renegotiating my relationship with my mother in another twenty or thirty years. The women whose losses occurred more than thirty years ago tell me how it's possible to live a full, happy, productive life in spite of this early trauma. They explain how a woman can move forward without leaving her mother behind.

This is not meant to be a book about how women should mourn. Instead, it's meant to be a book about the variety of ways that women *do* mourn. At lectures and seminars, I'm frequently asked to share my three- or four-step prescription for healthy mourning. "It's been five years since my mother died, and I don't feel that I've accepted her death yet," a young woman says. "What can I do to move on to that next stage of mourning?"

I wish I had a foolproof plan to offer. Although this book is structured according to how much time has elapsed since a mother's loss, I don't mean to imply that any kind of rigid schedule exists or should exist. Mourning is a highly individual process, its characteristics and intensity determined by the age a daughter was when her mother died, the cause of loss, the quality of the mother-daughter relationship, and the support system available both at the time of loss and in subsequent years. Instead of offering a step-by-step process for resolving one's grief, this book is meant to illustrate the varied experiences motherless daughters have as they mature and to shed some light on how the mourning process is likely to mutate and evolve over time. The best I can offer to women looking for a method is the assurance that when a woman is ready to mourn for her mother, she will. Trying to force oneself to take a step before its natural time can be as futile as trying to teach a newborn to walk.

It can take women years—and for some women, many years—to acknowledge, understand, and learn from the changes that have occurred as a result of early loss. A necessary part of a daughter's griefwork is acceptance—accepting that her life changed irrevocably when her mother died or left, and that she'll never be able to return to the child she was before. Death firmly shuts that door. As long as she resists this obvious and immutable truth, she'll continue struggling to find the peace she needs to successfully move on.

When I was traveling through the United States and Canada to promote *Motherless Daughters*, I came across the occasional critic who called in to a radio show or wrote a letter to a local newspaper describing the book as "just another example of women portraying themselves as victims." My gut response was typically one of outrage—as in, Who *is* this person? The Emotions Police? This book exists to help ease motherless women out of silence, not to force them back into it.

But after I'd heard from several of these callers

(do I even need to point out that most of them were men?) I began to feel less outraged than intrigued. I never intended to write a book about victimization, nor did I think of *Motherless Daughters* as a book about victims. I think of it—and of this book as well—as a compilation of stories about survivors. These are daughters who experienced the most profound loss a child can imagine, and who emerged intact and motivated to share their stories with other women who'd experienced the same.

It's true that some of the letters in this book detail the intense pain and struggles that some girls experience after losing their mothers, and that some writers have achieved a deeper degree of healing and insight than others. But it's also true that all of the daughters who speak here have tried to travel from a place of vulnerability and deprivation to a place of reflection and acceptance. The youngest girls have just begun this journey, and are uncertain of its future twists and turns. The most senior women describe how early mother loss influences the rest of a daughter's life. All of their letters tell stories of courage and hope and determination, stories that should stand as inspirations to us all.

# Letters from

# Motherless
# Daughters

*Chapter One*

# ADJUSTMENT AND ACCEPTANCE: THE FIRST FIVE YEARS

Not long ago, I was speaking to an audience of about eighty motherless daughters when a woman in the back of the room (we'll call her Allison) raised her hand. "Unlike most of you in this room, I just lost my mother four months ago," she explained, struggling to keep her voice steady. "I'm not yet at a point where I can even talk about it much. What I really want to know tonight is, When am I going to start feeling better? When does the pain finally go away?"

A woman seated off to my right turned toward Allison and said, "It *doesn't* ever go away, not completely. But it does change over time. You won't feel completely okay in another year, but I promise you will feel better."

Another woman (we'll call her Rosa) stood up and told the group, "I think the fact that we're all here tonight is proof that the hurt never stops. But I also think the fact that we're here tonight proves that you can get through this, and that even though the pain never goes away, you eventually *can* get on with your life." She turned toward Allison. "Let us be examples for you of women who've suffered this loss and survived."

Although Allison and Rosa have both lived through a similar loss, today they're experiencing motherlessness from opposite poles. Rosa, whose mother died twenty years ago, is more like the wise woman whose years of accumulated experience have given her the authority to act as a guide and a reference point for the newly motherless daughter. But Allison, only four months past the loss, is still in what psychologists call the "acute grief" phase or the "crisis grief" phase, which begins the moment the loss of a loved one occurs and ends only as we accept and start assimilating the reality of the loss.

This acute, or crisis, phase is typically characterized by several of the following responses: heightened anxiety; anger; depression; helplessness; irritability; restlessness; pining; persistent wishes to reverse the loss and obsessive thoughts of reunion; bargaining (with the lost loved one, or with God); a preoccupation with self-blame (characterized by "I should have . . ." or "If only I'd . . ."); decreased energy and motivation; sleep disturbances; weight loss or gain; fear of madness; a tendency to rely on cigarettes, drugs, or alcohol more than usual; and physical problems such as chest pains, stomach pains, or otherwise inexplicable symptoms. For many daughters, especially those who lost loved ones suddenly and unexpectedly, the acute grief phase may be filled with shock, numbness, denial, and blame.

In adults, this crisis period usually lasts for about six to eight months. That's one reason why many of us were told that we should be "over" a loss within six months, as if grief could be contained within such a rigidly prescribed period of time. Anyone who has suffered a significant loss as an adult knows that after six or eight months the initial daze does start to dissolve, but that hardly means the mourner's task is complete. Instead, the daughter who emerges from the crisis period finds she now has to get down to the very difficult job of confronting the painful reality of her loss.

For children and adolescents, the first six or eight months after a mother's death or departure may feel more like a period of disorganization and household chaos than like an acute emotional drain. That's because many children will wait until their surviving parent has passed through that critical, emotional period before allowing themselves to grieve. They're waiting until their new primary caregiver appears able to attend to their emotional needs. Even then, a daughter's capacity to mourn for her mother is directly proportional to two factors: the response of her surviving parent or primary caregiver, and the availability of a supportive environment in which she feels safe to express her sadness, anger, blame, or guilt. Ideally, that support system includes a surviving parent, siblings, family friends, and peers, but even one stable adult with a demonstrated interest in that child's well-being can help a daughter grieve to the best of her ability for her developmental stage. Daughters without such an adult may suppress or deny their true feelings for years, stuffing them under layers of stoicism and false maturity. It's not unheard of for a daughter to experience her acute grief phase ten or twenty years after her mother's death, when she finally feels stable enough within her own life to succumb to the intense emotions she's been suppressing for all that time.

As the letters from girls and women who've lost their mothers within the past year illustrate, those who've received emotional support from relatives or friends are the ones who seem best prepared to begin accepting the loss and moving on. In most of these daughters we see at least some evidence of acute grief symptoms: seventeen-year-old Kirsten writes of her shock and numbness; thirteen-year-old Jennifer describes her depression and difficulty keeping up in school; twenty-six-year-old Tina says she struggled with nighttime anxiety attacks for months.

The first full year after the loss of a mother requires a significant individual and family adjustment. No longer is Mom home to care for the younger siblings, offer support to her children, organize holiday celebrations, or keep Dad company. That initial twelve-month cycle also is important because it allows a family to experience a series of "firsts"—first Thanksgiving without Mom, first Christmas, first Mother's Day, first anniversary of her death—as an altered unit. When fathers begin dating seriously or remarry during this period, daughters often feel angry and resentful about having to accommodate a new family member so quickly or about feeling that they now have to experience each "first" alone.

As all these daughters quickly learned, early loss is a maturing experience. Even the youngest writers immediately began to think more expansively than others their age, describing their need to help other family members and their desire to find inner strength. Whatever the specific circumstances, the first twelve months or so after a mother's death are typically a chaotic, stressful time, as the following letters reveal.

• • •

## KIRSTEN,
*seventeen, whose mother died of cancer four months ago*

My mother died when I was seventeen, which seems ridiculous to say, since I am still seventeen. She died a scant four months ago. To be honest with you, it all seems so unreal. I can feel my heart ticking like a time bomb, and I know that sooner or later I will explode and everything that I am not feeling today will come hurtling to the surface.

I want to know if what I am feeling is normal. There is no one that I can talk to about this. After a little while, people don't think I have a problem; they assume that I've "gotten over it," when in all actuality I have not even grasped the fact that this is real. I have not yet lived long enough without my mother to realize what I am missing. I still expect to find her around every corner. I don't know if this is a normal reaction or if I'm just going crazy. Therapy is not an option, for I have no money.

Thank you for writing your book for people like me.

## ERIKA,

*sixteen, whose mother died during surgery four and a half months ago*

I'm a student at a high school for the performing arts, where I'm a vocal major. At the beginning of this past summer, I flew three thousand miles away to work in my uncle's coffeehouse. I went because things hadn't been going well between me and my parents during the past two years, and I told them in the spring that I wanted to get away from them for the summer. It was decided that I would spend the summer working for my uncle.

Two months earlier, my mother had told my older brother and me that she had fibroid tumors in her uterus and a few ovarian cysts. Her gynecologist told her that she would have to have a hysterectomy—not as soon as possible, but within the next few months.

I worked for my uncle for about two and a half weeks before I realized I just didn't want to be out there anymore. I couldn't think of a good reason why, but I just wanted to go back home so badly. I called my parents at 1:00 in the morning and asked them if I could come home. I had really missed them a lot, and realized I had left for the wrong reasons. When I talked to my mother, she was all groggy, but she was happy to hear that I wanted to come home. I made a reservation with the airline to go home the following Monday. Then I went to bed.

The next morning I talked to my father, and he seemed to have changed his mind. He told me to just give it another week. My mother agreed to this, too. I always do what my parents tell me to do, because I see no good reason to disobey them. So I called the airline and changed my flight. I kept that reservation, and when I landed at the airport, there was my mother, smiling, waiting for me at the gate. She held her arms out to me, and I hugged her for the last time. Then my father said we had to go to the baggage claim.

The next morning at 9:00 my mother was scheduled to have surgery, not to have an actual hysterectomy but to just have the fibroids and cysts removed. I slept late that morning, till about 11:00. That afternoon was a hazy, balmy one, and I wandered around feeling shitty about myself because I had no idea how I was going to spend the rest of the summer. I went home around 2:30. When I got home, there wasn't much to do but unpack. I sat in front of the TV in the living room unpacking. It was raining outside, and I felt so crappy.

Around 4:45 or so, my brother and my father came home. They came into the living room looking very serious. My brother turned off the TV and sat down on the chair at the other side of the room. My father sat down next to me on the couch and took my hands. He said to me, "She's gone. We lost her."

I immediately burst into tears.

It turns out that the surgery itself had gone okay, but while the doctor was sewing her back up, her blood pressure dropped and she lost her vital signs. The heart team worked on her for more than an hour trying to resuscitate her. Nothing.

It didn't take long to spread the word. By Friday of that week, enough people knew so that more than 250 showed up for her memorial service. Two of my mother's best friends and her boss gave eulogies.

But it was before the service that I saw her. I saw her lying in that casket and just got so angry. My mother, in all her beauty, in all her greatness, in all her wit, wisdom, skill, and integrity, had been reduced to a pile of flesh. I cried hysterically and my brother held me as he bawled, too.

Death is the most undignified thing there is. God is mean for doing it to us. My wonderful, hard-working mother was now dead. All through the service I begged God to please take her and make her alive again, somehow. If it was to be in heaven, fine. Anywhere, just as long as she represented more than that pile of flesh.

That was a little over four months ago. I was still fifteen then. My mother was forty-nine. We still don't know exactly what went wrong, but we don't really care yet. The fact that she's dead is enough to try to swallow, never mind how it happened.

I started my junior year of high school this September, and went on with my life, minus my mother. I see the same therapist I've been seeing since last spring. I'm very close with my guidance counselor, too. I take acting classes, and I'm trying as hard as I can to do well in school. My friends and neighbors have been very nice to me.

My brother has his own apartment about an hour away. He'll be twenty-one this month. I see him once every two weeks or so.

Our house is messy and quiet. But I'm not afraid to be here. I can't be. So many things in my life seem broken up and chaotic, everything except my will to be successful, my inner strength, and my hope. I want to be a great actress someday. That's my dream, and the more I am bombarded with the reminder of mortality, the more I think my dream will come true.

### JENNIFER,
*thirteen, whose mother died of cancer seven months ago*

I'm thirteen years old and I'm in junior high. Recently, four parents of kids in my school have passed away. Two of these deaths were caused by cancer.

One of these was my mom. She died in December of last year. Now I live with my aunt, and I try to be as considerate as possible. When my mother died, I didn't know what to do. My grades went down, I was depressed all the time, and I just felt like everything was going wrong. I got help from many people—counselors, teachers, people at my church. Nothing seemed to help. But with God's help I have managed to go on with my life. I have to, for my little brother and my little sister. Now I'm much better, but it still worries me.

Many teenagers take their mothers for granted. I want them to understand they shouldn't. When my mom was getting more and more ill, I told her as many times as I could that I loved her and that she was the best. It's very hard for a person like me to say nice things, but she was my mother and she was dying. I hope that other teens don't have to go through all that to be able to say "I love you" to a parent. Because you can't turn time back.

SHERYL,
*twenty-one, whose mother died five months ago*

My mom died this past winter, and I can truly say that my family was torn apart by her death. My dad now lives 1,100 miles away and has a new girlfriend.

Normally, I give people a chance, but I can't stand the thought of my dad dating. (He's not exactly keen about any of my dates—he calls all of them Herkimer!) Meanwhile, I run our family business by myself while trying to stay in college. I get so lonely without anyone around.

I never regretted not having siblings before, because Mom and I did stuff together. Every Sunday night we went to the movies and dinner. I just turned twenty-one last month and really regret that I didn't spend more time with her. But I'm really glad I had the chance to become friends with her. If she had died when I was in high school . . . well, there was a lot of tension between us then.

I want to thank you for addressing an issue that I've discovered *no one* wants to deal with.

**LORI,**
*fifteen, whose mother died of leukemia seven months ago*

My mother was diagnosed with leukemia after a month-long bout with gingivitis. I learned that she had cancer while driving home with my two brothers and my father from my Bat Mitzvah rehearsal dinner. My mother was transferred to the hospital where my father works as a gastroenterologist. I cried almost every night, terrified of what was happening to my mother and what the consequences would be. My mother was not even able to attend my Bat Mitzvah because the doctors did not want her to catch any unnecessary germs.

My mother came home for a month to prepare herself for a bone marrow transplant, which occurred at a hospital six hundred miles away. I saw my mom twice in the next three months. In that time period, her hair completely fell out and was replaced by a wig. During the time when my mother was away, I was suddenly burdened with responsibilities that I had taken for granted when my mother was healthy: feeding the dog, making my lunch, changing my sheets, making dinner, watching my brothers. Four months later, my mother's health suddenly declined. She had suffered through the bone marrow transplant, countless doses of chemotherapy, and much more. I was over at a friend's house when their telephone rang. It was a close family friend calling to tell me that my mother had lapsed into a coma. I remember the whole world going black as I kneeled down on my friend's kitchen floor, sobbing with the knowledge that my mother was going to die.

That night was the worst night of my life. I hardly slept the entire night, but paced the hallways with anxiety. I prayed to God to save my mother, to not let her die. My brothers and I were so young . . . we needed her. Twenty-four hours after she had fallen into a coma, my mother woke up. Her recovery from it was rapid, and within a few days she could sit up and talk. She continued to come home for short periods of time, almost every weekend, until one week she went back into the hospital and stayed there. Nine months after her diagnosis, my mother died in the hospital. My brothers were six and twelve, and I was fourteen.

Although I went to school the day after she died, I wasn't prepared for the sympathetic looks and somber whisperings of my classmates. I went home early. I went to the funeral service for my mother, but I didn't go to the cemetery. I wasn't prepared to see my mother, my once energetic, loving, beautiful mother placed into a box and lowered into the ground.

Both my brothers and I have recently started to go to counseling. I find it very helpful, as well as writing in my diary. As a result of my mother's death, my family has become closer. I now confide in my father. Before my mother's death, I only saw him from 6:30 P.M. until 9:00 P.M. every night. I also realize that I am lucky, despite my mother's death. It sounds funny to say that there has been some good that came out of this tragedy, but there has. I learned a lot during the period of her illness. As my mother told me one day before she went into the hospital for the first time, "You may not always hear me, but you'll always feel my answer."

## VALERY,

*sixteen, whose mother died in a car accident eight months ago*

I can relate to what you are feeling and what you mean when you say, "I know what a real crisis is now." You said you thought about that when you failed a test or something. That is exactly the way that I feel now when I fail at doing something. You also described your house as empty and silent after your mother died. That is also the way our house is. I know all of this because my mom died in November last year. Not a very nice Thanksgiving for our family.

Since my mother has been gone, many people have come up to me and said, "Oh, you must be happy that your mother is gone," or "You look a lot like your mom." I want my mom to be remembered as her, and I want to be remembered as myself. Also, I'm *not* happy that my mother is gone, even though I didn't agree with some of the stuff she did. I loved her anyway. I still love her.

## TINA,

*twenty-six, whose mother died of cancer one year ago*

My beautiful mom, Susan, died last year at the much-too-young age of forty-six. I never got to say a real good-bye to her because the asshole doctors kept telling us she was going to make it until she finally had to be put on a respirator and it was too late. From the time we found out she had a tumor in her lung to the time she died was about three weeks. My dad is now forty-nine (and already engaged!) and I have a ten-year-old sister. (She's adopted, so she's now lost two mothers.)

My mom's death was the most horrible thing that has ever happened to me. Even though I am a constant worrier, I never once considered that she would die. After her death, I had to do things I wouldn't wish on anyone. I had to tell my little sister that our mom was dead—all I remember is her gut-wrenching shriek and when I said our mom's heart gave out, her screaming, "Why couldn't they have given her a pig's heart?" I had to write her obituary. I had to collect her clothes for the funeral home and pick out her coffin and flowers. I had to clean out her closet.

My mom had me when she was only twenty-one. She said we all "grew up together." We were best friends and would talk on the phone almost every day. She always talked about how we would be little old ladies together. She couldn't wait until my husband and I had a baby. She was a genuinely wonderful woman with a wacky sense of humor and the kindest heart. One thousand people came to her funeral.

She used to get up in the middle of the night instinctually when I was sick, hold my hair back when I was throwing up, and get me a glass of Pepsi to get rid of the bad taste. When I was little, she would tell me that she would never let anything bad happen to me. She told me stories about moms who, with adrenaline, would lift cars to save their children and said she would do that for me, too. When my husband and I moved into our first apartment, she came over to scrub out all the cabinets and help me set up the kitchen. When I was reading my poetry at a coffeehouse, she got all dressed up in a black turtleneck and came to hear me—sipping decaf and sitting in a rickety chair, making conversation with all the café types—she was so proud. She was just that kind of mom, and sometimes I can't believe she's never coming back.

When she died, even though I had never been to a therapist before, I knew that this was really bad and I wouldn't be able to make it on my own. I thought I'd go for a few sessions and get it all straightened out, but ha—I soon realized I was in a bottomless pit of grief. It's only now, after a year, that the therapist thinks I can take a little break from my weekly visits.

I was in horrible shape. I cried every night until I could barely breathe, and my husband would get up to get me half a Xanax (ever so thoughtfully provided by the hospital when my mom died). Work meant nothing to me. I was really hurt when my dad started dating a woman a month after my mom's funeral and expected me to be happy for him. I felt horrible grief and guilt trying to take care of my little sister as best I could while maintaining my own life—taking her to a sex-ed class at her school when it should have been my mom, buying her underwear when I realized she had outgrown it all, cutting her fingernails, begging her to write thank-you notes so no one would think she didn't have manners, and just making sure she didn't look like a pitiful orphan. I felt like no one understood. People tried to be nice, especially friends of my mother, but everyone eventually goes back to their routine and you still have to deal with the mess.

Like you, I looked for an appropriate book in countless bookstores. I'm that kind of person. When I don't know how to do something, I'll read a book. There was nothing on this. The [Elisabeth] Kübler-Ross stuff pissed me off. The New Age stuff depressed me. Books about angels comforted me in a small way, but I wanted a guidebook to tell me what to expect—to tell me what to do with a million pairs of my mother's shoes, to tell me what to do with her bras, to tell me what to do when none of the relatives wanted to come over to the house for Christmas because they said it was too depressing.

Your book talks to the loneliest, most private void in my heart. It tells me that I'm not a freak with an abnormal attachment to my mother because I'm still grieving after a year. It tells me that all my feelings and experiences (suddenly not wanting a baby, insisting on wearing my mom's twenty-five-year-old hippie poncho, hating cute older women I see in the market, etc.) are pretty normal, or at least that other people have gone through them.

I will admit that my mom's death had some good points, if you could call them that. I have a new, mature relationship with my father, small things don't stress me out anymore, I am more passionate about everything—I really appreciate a beautiful day, good food, friends, my husband—and I have finally formed a "family unit" with my husband that exists independently of my dad and sister.

I don't want my mom's life to have been in vain. She never went to college, but was incredibly bright and read voraciously. She wanted so much for me. Even though it never would have come to that, she said she would wait tables to put me through college, and I know she would've. This is one of the things that haunts me: she was really creative and thinking about going to a gemology college to learn to make jewelry, but didn't go because she thought $7,000 was too expensive. I later saw the check my dad wrote to the funeral home and mortuary to pay for everything—it was $7,000. Sick irony.

Do I still hurt? Yes, and I always will. There is so much stuff that I want to ask her! I want to dial the house and have her pick up the phone. I want to hear her laugh. I want to hug her. I want to give her a beautiful grandchild to spoil. I want her to smooth my hair the way she did. Oh, I could go on and on. You know the rest. . . . The stories are all the same.


## ELAINE,
*forty, whose mother died of cancer one year ago*

I'm an adopted child, and for the past twenty-one years I lived with my adoptive mother. I might add that for the most part we lived as friends. You see, I missed what I felt would have been a very important part of my life. During my teens, my parents divorced, and I was unable to understand that my mother was having as difficult a time as I was. The family was split apart, and there was a great deal of bitterness on both sides. My mother and I butted heads, and I was already more mature than my years in a lot of ways, but perhaps not in the ways that may have really counted and would have helped me to get through the situation that we were all facing.

I moved in with my father when I was thirteen years old. I was an oddity, and was thought very strangely of, as my father was a salesman and was out of town a lot. I was left to my own devices. It certainly could have been a fiasco for my father, but I was much more mature than my years. During that time, I didn't realize what a hard time my mother was having. She was struggling to put her life to-gether, had sold her home, and was renting a home and pursuing her artwork. I was really pissed off with her because she didn't come to my high school graduation. It wasn't until I was eighteen and already married that I realized how much I loved her and missed her. She was very ill at that time—I didn't know how ill until afterwards. The rest of the family made it a point to keep me informed but not to emphasize just how serious it really was. Their fear was that I would come home and she would realize she was dying, for there would certainly be no other reason for me to come that far, as I was just married and had really no money to speak of. They thought she would have given up the fight.

She was hospitalized for thirty-three days. Dur-ing that time the doctors had informed her parents three different times not to go home, that she wasn't going to make it through the night. What a hellacious situation for her parents, and yet their thoughts were to protect both her and me.

Already, my husband and I were having some problems and thought that perhaps one way to resolve them might be to move. I asked my mother if we could come to her home. This was only months after her serious health situation. She had absolutely no reservations and allowed us to come to her home. She never set a time limit as to how long we could stay—her home was our home. The marriage didn't last, and she helped me pick up the pieces. It wasn't long afterward that she was hospitalized again and I realized that I might lose her. I had already felt as though I'd lost her during those years between the ages of thirteen and eighteen. I just wasn't ready for this.

We became so very close just before the surgery. I had always wanted that closeness from her. She wasn't always able to give it, as she hadn't been given it as a child. She had been raised in different homes until about the age of ten.

For the next several years, her health was not the best, but she did very little complaining. I was always the one who was worried about her and would push her to go to the doctor when I was certain she wasn't feeling well. She was there for me when I found a lump in my right breast at the age of twenty-three. She went with me to the doctor, waited for me, talked to the doctor and explained that I was very scared, and asked him to prescribe something so that I would at least be able to sleep until the results came back. I had several other surgeries as time went by, including the one where I decided I didn't want to have children. My mother was a woman who was unable to have children and had wanted me and adopted me, yet she stood by the decision I made. She kept my secrets. She was my best friend.

My mother hung in there with me when I had bouts of depression, or when some stupid man was in my life and I was allowing him to make me miserable. I was always an overweight child, and she never allowed anyone to call me fat. I finally decided to go through Weight Watchers and lost a substantial amount of weight. It took me two years to do it, but she was there all the way, helping me keep up the fight.

When I was twenty-one, she encouraged me to seek out my biological mother and gave me every bit of information that she could recall. After I received a letter from my biological mother, she drove me to the airport, even though she was terrified of driving there, with all the traffic and her fear of getting lost. We cried and said good-bye—she, fearful that I wouldn't come back; me, fearful that she wouldn't want me to, as though I had betrayed her in some way. I was never so glad to get home as I was after that trip to visit my biological mother, Beverly. I swore then that although Beverly had given birth to me, the woman I called "Mom" and would always call "Mom" had given me life.

My mother left me two days before her seventy-first birthday and two weeks before my fortieth. When we knew that she wasn't going to have much longer, she asked me to take her home. The hardest thing that I have ever done was to bring my mother home to let her die.

I have never felt as lonely as I have these past months without her. My best friend is gone. I know that the grieving and this emptiness I feel, this gaping hole in the pit of my soul, is not something that is going away easily. Although it will perhaps take a lifetime to get over this loss, I am learning to celebrate the joy in all the things that she left me. I know that she left me her green thumb, and the house that we shared for so long I've made my own, which I know she would have wanted. I still hear her voice, calling to me to come see a beautiful sunset that she was observing while painting a Christmas card for someone special. It's almost that time of year now, and I will miss the smell of cookies that she always baked. She loved this time of year so. She would start to decorate the house around Thanksgiving and would insist that I get her a tree for Christmas.

The last year of my mother's life was a strange one for me, at best. I started to experience a lot of stress, which caused me a great deal of pain in the chest area. I was frantic, which just seemed to exacerbate the problem. This started about two years ago and continued until about two months ago. The doctor I was seeing for this problem sent me to a psychologist. At the time, I had no idea that my mother had lung cancer. It didn't become evident to me until two weeks before she died. She had managed to keep it a secret for that long. My doctor's nurse thinks that perhaps somehow I knew about my mother's condition, because there didn't seem to be a medical reason for my chest pains.

I still see a therapist at this point, and I'm trying very hard to put things together in my life. I know that I was very fortunate to have had my mother. She was no saint, and certainly neither am I. I am just very lucky to have had a best friend like her. The real point of all this is to say it doesn't really matter how old you are. The loss of a mother hurts—hurts terribly. It doesn't matter the age.

• • •

Daughters who pass through the crisis phase of grief find that the acute pain and denial begin to decrease.

They slowly move beyond the searching that's so common to the initial grief process. Their failure to achieve a reunion with their lost mothers helps them begin to realize and accept that their mothers are truly gone.

Some residue of disbelief and resistance may persist at this time, but these responses no longer mandate the course of a daughter's day. The impulse to pick up the telephone and call a mother has transformed into the wish that the mother could be called. Twenty-one-year-old Sherri, whose mother died after surgery four years ago, describes how her grief has evolved since her mother died:

> For the entire year after her death, maybe even longer, she was all I could think about. Whenever I made a new acquaintance, I had the urge to blurt out, "My mother is dead," as if I were hiding something from them by not providing that information. When I went into drugstores, cards "For that Special Mother" attacked me as I walked down the aisle. I spent many afternoons and nights—too many—locked in my dorm room, playing Neil Diamond, a favorite of Mom's, crying into my teddy bear as I stared with disbelief and despair at my favorite picture of our family.
>
> It's nearly impossible to believe that I'm a

senior in college and that it's been four years since my mother's death. The pain has never subsided completely—it never will—but I no longer wear it on my sleeve.

As the psychiatrist Vamik Volken explains in his 1993 book, *Life after Loss*, a daughter moves into the second stage of mourning when she accepts her loss. Then she begins what he calls "the subtle and complex negotiations" required for her to integrate the memory of her mother into her motherless life. This process often involves an attempt to make sense of the loss, and to fit it into her life story in a meaningful way. Most daughters whose losses occurred one to five years ago, like twenty-one-year-old Sherri and twenty-six-year-old Jean, find they're still searching for that meaning. The platitudes and clichés—such as "God must have needed another angel"—that may have sustained a daughter at first feel less satisfying now. She wants weightier explanations for her pain.

After two or three years, when the shock and numbness have passed, daughters may feel the effects of blocking or suppressing the emotions that were too frightening for a child to allow herself to feel at the time. Thirteen-year-old Jewel, whose mother died of cancer four years ago, writes:

> When I was only nine, my mother died.
> Unlike you and your mom who liked to go

shopping, my mom and I didn't have our "thing" we did together. That is what I miss the most: knowing that one day we could have talked and laughed together like friends, not just as parent and child.

It didn't really hit me that I lost my mom until years later. I remember that I didn't even cry when I saw her lifeless body in the hospital. Now, I wish that I had cried then. Maybe it would have helped me now.

By this point, even the youngest girls already can see that mourning will not end quickly, and perhaps will not end at all. For those who find this realization too difficult to bear, a dependence on alcohol or drug use or other harmful behaviors established during the acute grief phase may blossom into a full-blown addiction. Other daughters become determined to find a way to learn from their loss and to apply these lessons to their daily lives. Twenty-nine-year-old Ellen wants to become more self-reliant and trust her own intuition. Twenty-one-year-old Sherri is trying to assess what is most meaningful about life and is looking for a way to integrate this philosophy with her long-term plans. Their next steps will be to decide how to reach these new goals, and to establish themselves as independent women, without feeling as if they've left their mothers behind.

. . .

# ALEXIS,

*thirteen, whose mother died suddenly two years ago*

My mother died when I was eleven years old. I walked into the living room and found her lying on the couch. Her death was a complete shock to me. She had seemed healthy before.

My mother and I used to fight a lot, and I would say, "I hate you." I know that hurt her so much. I never meant it. I hope she knows that.

The hardest part about my mother's death was going back to school. Kids in my fifth grade class brought me presents, like stuffed animals. I accepted them, but wondered why. My entire class made me cards. Even my teacher gave us no work so I wouldn't have any.

The one difference between your family and mine was that mine grew closer and became more dependent on each other. My brother and I started to have long talks. They really helped me. My dad had to work a lot, so my brother and I became loners, in a way.

There are constant reminders of my mother wherever I go. She *still* gets mail and phone calls, and people at my school are always saying, "Let your mom sign this." I know I will never get over her, but I have to get on with my life.

## LYNN,
*eighteen, whose mother died in a car accident a year and a half ago*

My mother died suddenly when I was sixteen. After her death, my family completely changed. We got much closer, but her loss was a real blow to me because life was great until the day she was killed. Everything I see or do reminds me of something she said or did, or even the way she spoke with an accent, even today, a year and a half later.

After her death, I was forced to become an independent adult, and I started spinning aimlessly. I found it hard to live the way I was used to. I spent all of my time with friends so I wouldn't let myself have time to think. Unfortunately, I also didn't give myself time to eat. I slowly developed anorexia nervosa, even though I didn't realize what was happening to me. It was only a month ago that I started recovering from it.

I guess I felt that my mother always wanted me to be perfect, so I would become perfect for her after her death as a gift. I didn't realize how thin I was, even when I dropped from a size 12 to a size 8. My friends were worried about me when I didn't eat lunch at school, but I would always just tell them that I liked to eat when I got home—but I never did. I just wish I could be like any other normal person. Sometimes I feel like I'm going crazy, but I talk to my sister (who's also my best friend) and she usually comforts me. I try to remember that motherless doesn't mean parentless. I still have my father, even though he always worked when I was growing up so I never even knew him before my mother died. I'm hoping that in the future I will get on with my life and live for the future, not in the past.

## PAULETTE,
*thirty-seven, whose mother died a year and a half ago*

Although my mother died when I was thirty-five, I was an only child and we were extremely close. I was an adult when she died (although I wonder, because I don't really feel "grown up"), but I very much feel the feelings you've described. I also feel a sort of double loss because she had me when she was forty years old, so was sort of a mother and a grandmother at the same time (since I never knew either of my grandparents). Because of this, I am also experiencing this loss from the perspective of my three very young children, who will never be blessed with having really known my mother. My oldest was five and a half when she died.

For months after my mother's death I would start to cry every time I entered the car to drive anywhere—whether to pick up my child from school, go to the market, etc. The experience became so debilitating that I sought professional help. My therapist's explanation and proposed solution was so helpful to me that I wanted to share it with you.

First, he suggested that I was crying in this manner because I was not allowing myself time to grieve (because I just had too much to do with three small children). "It" was just spilling over and out of me whenever it had the chance—for example, when I was alone in the car. He proposed that I allow myself this seemingly purposeless time, which was so important. But what helped me the most was when he also proposed that I must be feeling an enormous burden, being the only child of now two deceased parents. It was *my* responsibility alone to carry on whatever legacies would be carried on from the existence of my parents, since I was the only one who really lived the experience. This feeling was truly overwhelming. His next suggestion saved my sanity—it gave me permission to grieve in a way that I did not worry was "wasting my time." He said that it might help to put together a book for my children about my mother and father with photos, stories, and facts. In this way, I would be doing a service to my children by helping them understand their roots, and at the same time I would be spending time thinking about them and getting through some grieving that way. I must tell you that since that day, I have never cried again in the car.

JEAN,
*twenty-six, whose mother died of cancer two years ago*

My mother died when I was twenty-four. I'm an only child and have always been extremely independent; now I find that I have more of a sense of separation anxiety than I've ever felt before. It's rather unnerving to be twenty-six and suddenly feeling a shaky foundation where I've never felt one before.

It has greatly affected my romantic relationships in that I have never wanted to feel "tied down" or "stuck" with one man. Now, I'm terrified to be alone, terrified to lose my boyfriend of two and a half years. Yet at the same time I know that the harder I try to hold onto him, the more I'm hurting our relationship. I'm afraid of being left alone by another person I love so dearly, especially if I can "control" this—our relationship. See, I couldn't control her cancer.

I constantly tell myself that there was a reason for her early death . . . and that someday I'll know that answer. I tell myself that "only the good die young" (she was forty-eight). Or I push it all out of my mind when I'm feeling too emotionally drained to deal with it on some days. The knowledge of the reality that she will not be picking up the phone when I'm calling my father, or dropping what she's doing so that she can talk with me is often heart-breaking. I miss being able to call her at work and just say, "Hi! I was thinking of you."

I work for a family, and I'm privy to a lot of personal confrontations amongst my employers and their children. When I witness one of the arguments between the eldest daughter and her mother, my heart just breaks. It's not my place to intervene, but my mind's often racing as they're arguing. I want to grab the daughter by the shoulders and say to her, "Hey! It's your *mother* you're yelling at! Why are you wasting such precious time with her by screaming? Enjoy this time—be friends! Because it's all over before you know it."

Pretty crazy, I'm sure. But that's how I feel. I guess it's true to say that, at times, I'm envious of the time and experiences some girls have with their mothers. I would do anything to spend time with mine again, and it hurts me to see people taking for granted *their* time with their loved ones.

It would mean the world to me just to—once again—see my mother smile at me, touch me, and say my name, one last time.

## ELLEN,

*twenty-nine, whose mother died of hepatitis three years ago*

I lost my mom when I was twenty-six. She was an operating-room nurse, and several years before that had been pricked by a needle that was infected with the disease.

As I became an adult, my mom became a child. I was never able to relate to her on a mature, adult level. I was dispensing medication and changing diapers. I was taxi driver, cook, maid—everything but a daughter. I was in college when she was first diagnosed, and until she died, I lived and breathed the disease. I didn't date. I didn't go out very much. I gained weight.

When Mom passed away, it was peaceful because she was no longer in pain. I had mourned the loss before she died and thought I was done. I now know I am not. I recently ended a relationship after two and a half years, and I feel abandoned. I should've been way out of it shortly after meeting Allan, but I didn't want to lose another person I loved. He had some problems, so being a caretaker, I saw him as someone else to take care of. He was horrible to me, but it was better than losing something I had put so much time, effort, heart, and money into.

I didn't have the best relationship with my mom. So when Allan treated me poorly, I thought, "Okay. My mother showed her love this way. Allan acts this way. He must love me!" Well, after two and a half years I finally realize love is not supposed to hurt.

Being a caretaker has made it hard for me to let go. I want to be taken care of! I'm trying to break the pattern of putting others before myself. I did it for so long. Now it's time for me. When I was ready to be taken care of, Allan wasn't ready to care. Losing my mom has made me realize that I need to be my own support, my own guide, my own best friend.

## HELEN,

*twenty-six, whose mother died in an airplane crash four years ago*

As I begin this letter, my dad is on his way here to go to a baseball game with me. Coincidentally, today is also the first anniversary of my grandmother's death to cancer.

Four years ago, my mother and her mother died in a plane crash in Costa Rica while on vacation. I had just turned twenty-two. My dad's mother's death last year made all of my feelings of loss come rushing back. I think my sisters and I turned all of our needs for a maternal figure onto Gram. She was eighty-five and in no position to be a mother to us, but she was there to spoil us and to love us unconditionally. She always had been. And maybe four years is not a lot of time to deal with all of this death.

I had a wonderful childhood. We grew up in the house that my dad still lives in. I am the middle of three girls, and close to both of my sisters.

Two years ago, my older sister, my mom's brother, and I went to Costa Rica to see the airplane and meet the emergency room team that went out to the mountain when the plane crashed. All three of us had high hopes of putting this behind us once we saw the plane.

We met the men who were there the morning of the crash. They graciously took a day off of work and drove us up into the mountains to see the plane. Our first stop was a small coffee plantation several miles from the actual crash. Our "guide," Ricardo, introduced us to the farmer. The farmer pointed to a large piece of metal on top of a box in his backyard. Ricardo explained that it was a wing from the plane. The farmer had heard of the crash (it was the first crash in Costa Rica in forty years) and wandered toward it until he found something useful—a roof for his chicken coop.

That was a shock. I had so many emotions running through me. Mostly, I was angry and insulted. Maybe it was a warm-up for actually seeing the plane. It really forced me back into reality. No longer did I think that the whole world knew and cared about my mom and grandmother dying so needlessly. One of the guys recognized my mom from a picture we had brought of her. He was the person who actually pulled her out of the plane after the crash. As I look back on our trip, my obsession with these details really was my way of avoiding the griefwork that needed to be done.

## SHERRI,
*twenty-one, whose mother died after surgery four years ago*

I lost my mother, very suddenly, when I was seventeen. She was forty-two when she died due to complications from brain surgery that was supposed to remove an aneurism.

Before my mother died, we were a happy, typical all-American family living in the Midwest, and I really didn't know how lucky I was. Perhaps I'm being too hard on myself, but when I try to think of memories of me and my mom, I remember that I was a brat much of the time. Everyone assures me that "she knew how much you loved her," but sometimes I wonder. I am stubborn like my father in that I like to handle things myself, without depending on other people. One day I gave in and started to read a book on grief by C. S. Lewis. His theory was that the deceased person for whom we mourn does not look over us for the rest of our lives, as I had been assured. Friends and family repeated, "She'll always be with you," countless times when I was in despair. According to Lewis, this would be too painful for the deceased person, to watch the life that was stolen from them continue without them. This theory troubled me so much that I stopped reading those kinds of do-it-yourself grief books. I knew that I could not survive if I didn't believe that Mom could hear me talk and watch me live.

A favorite comfort of my dad is to tell me that Mom gave me everything I need to live a wonderful life. The way she influenced and loved me in such a short time is more than most people receive in a lifetime. I know this is true, but it never serves as much of a comfort. Why did God take her away when I wasn't done with her yet? I still spend hours trying to find the answer to this question. Maybe some angels needed her warmth and compassion to save thousands of children. No, that's not good enough. I don't care about those children. She's *my* mom. Why couldn't God choose someone else's mother? With all the cruel people in this world who contribute nothing but pain to others, why did God steal a person who embodied the concept of love? I had always lived by the idea that everything happens for a reason. But what could possibly be the reason for this? Was God trying to punish me? There surely were other ways I could learn to do more household chores than to have to do them because Mom is gone. Maybe if Mom had lived, something would have happened to cause her great pain and suffering, so God took her painlessly to prevent that. Today, this is still the explanation that I cling to most often.

Perhaps finding the explanation is less important than learning how to deal with the consequences. I still have faith that Mom is with me everywhere that I go. Sometimes I like to close my eyes and deceive myself into imagining that she is *really* with me. I imagine hugging her again. I picture her visiting me at college with my dad, meeting my roommates and all of the people in my life who will never have the privilege of knowing her. I can't help thinking that if she is watching me from heaven, she is probably very sad to be away. Dad always insists that he never feels sorry for himself, as devastated as he is to have lost his wife. "The person I feel sorry for is your mother," he says, with tears in his eyes. "She doesn't get to be with her children as they grow up."

My constant mourning has lessened over the years, but an incredible fear of death seems to have taken its place. The thought of death horrifies me. My only comfort is the hope that I will be reunited with my mother. This fear of death has begun to play an increasingly important role in how I live my life. It has caused me to think very seriously about what is meaningful. I'll never forget that I was too busy studying to realize that Mom was having surgery the next day. I didn't have the perspective to understand that my schoolwork should have been sacrificed to spend more time with her. Now, the people I love are more important to me than books and papers are. Still, I know a person cannot live entirely by this attitude. I'm constantly debating whether to live for now or to prepare for the future. I suppose every person must find a way to balance the two, but I've never been very good at balancing things.

I'm not sure that I have accepted Mom's death entirely, but I have tried to live as full a life as possible for the past four years, and I'll continue to do so. My father has always encouraged me to look for the positive in every situation. Well, Dad, this is a tough one. Four years later, I still can't come up with even one positive consequence that holds any weight. I have decided, however, that living my life as fully as my mother did, by continuing to use her as my example, is a way to avoid adding to the negativity of her absence.

I continue to be confused, sad, angry, and scared, often all at once. I desperately wish I could speak to her one more time. I can feel her presence beside me now, and I can only have faith that she feels my love.

Not long ago, I wrote her the following letter:

Dear Mom,

How's the weather in heaven? Is it sunny? It's been kind of cloudy lately here. I was just thinking about you and thought I'd write. I really miss you, Mom. My life is going really well and I wish you could be a part of it. The other day I jogged by where you and Dad and I used to live. I was too young to remember that house, but I remember the playground you used to take me to. It seems a lot smaller now. I visited you at the cemetery once around Christmas, and I'm sorry I didn't go again. It's just that I don't picture you there. I picture you alive and with me every day. Please make a special effort to be with me this Monday when I take my exam on the Bible; I could use some inside information. I love you, Mom. Please look over Dad and Paul; I don't think they let you know how they feel as openly as I do. Give my love to Jupiter and Mozart. The house seemed empty without Jupiter's barking, and I still miss Mozart's chirping. I feel better knowing they're with you. I envy them for that. Please keep in touch and let me know when you receive this letter—I'm not sure about the postage.

Love always,
Sherri

*Chapter Two*

# PAIN TURNS TO LONGING: FIVE TO TEN YEARS

I suspect I'm not the best example of adjustment and acceptance after a mother's death, since my story of grieving begins here. At the seven-year mark, to be exact. Until then, I'd avoided feeling much sadness, despair, anger, guilt, or remorse. Instead, I focused on being the bravest little soldier in my family's army of four. Whenever an intense emotion threatened to emerge, I forcefully pushed it back. Success was remarkably straightforward: if I didn't allow myself to think or talk about my mother, I didn't get upset. Outfitted with a phony smile and a deliberately vacant gaze, I acted like a Chatty Cathy doll that repeated the same sentence over and over when my string was pulled: "I'm doing fine, thank you."

I've read that losing a loved one is like breaking a bone: if the bone isn't set properly it'll eventually heal on its own, but it'll cause pain throughout the rest of your life. To ease that pain you have to break the bone again and reset it properly. In much the same way, a daughter who forcefully resists grieving for her mother will be able to function to some degree, but she'll never feel emotionally whole until she revisits the loss and allows herself to feel its accompanying pain.

Gloria Steinem once said that for years she believed she could keep a wall between herself and her childhood, only to discover what a faulty construction that was. Seven years after my mother's death, I found it impossible—not to mention exhausting—to maintain such a Berlin Wall between myself and my emotions for any longer. The wall, quite simply, collapsed one afternoon. Which is how I wound up at the age of twenty-four, doubled over in the middle of a street as cars whizzed by and crying for my mother, finally able to feel what I'd not been able to feel at seventeen.

I've met several motherless women who identify seven years as the lag time between their mothers' deaths and the inception of their mourning processes. I was familiar with seven-year cycles in nature and in social anthropology (such as the "seven-year itch"); but why would so many daughters wait seven years before grieving for a mother? Only when I noticed that all of these women were adolescents at the time of loss did this seven-year lapse seem like more than mere coincidence.

For most teenage daughters who lose their mothers, a five- to ten-year period offers adequate time to achieve independence from the nuclear family. Many daughters are forced into a state of *emotional* independence after their mothers die, but remain financially or socially dependent on their close relatives or caregivers until their early to mid-twenties. At that time, they're likely to make the transition to a family or a job of their own, and establish a home base that doesn't involve relatives for the first time.

Only when a daughter feels secure within her own life, when she's free from daily ties to her family members and doesn't have to worry about their reactions to her grief (including being cut off from the family for speaking about the unspeakable), will she feel safe enough to mourn. For me, that time arrived during my twenty-fourth year. I'd just experienced another profound loss—the breakup of an engagement—but this time I had a secure job and a close group of friends who I knew would provide me with a safety net if I fell. When mourning the loss of my fiancé and the plans we'd had together sent me right back to mourning for my mother, I was ready to face the pain. Intense emotion felt like much less of a threat to me at twenty-four than it had at seventeen.

The five- to ten-year postloss period carries women who were adolescents and young adults when their mothers died into years that may include marriage, childbirth, or other transitional times when a motherless woman deeply misses her mother and yearns for her guidance and care. Letters from daughters who lost their mothers between five and ten years ago reveal that even adult daughters feel vulnerable and long to be taken care of. Twenty-six-year-old Lynn is struggling to recapture the sense of self-worth she says she lost nine years ago when her mother died from cancer. Thirty-one-year-old Beth Ann yearns to call her mother for advice about raising her young child.

Daughters who were twelve years old or younger when their mothers died enter or even complete adolescence during the next five to ten years. One of the most important tasks of the teen years is to develop an independent identity, and to achieve this a girl needs a woman to measure herself against and separate from. When a mother is not present, a daughter may act out against a father or an older sister instead. Some daughters turn their rebellion inward, acting out with alcohol, food, or drugs. Daughters who are immersed in the mother's role of caretaker for the family may bypass their rebellion phase completely and later resent family members for "stealing" their identities.

During a motherless girl's adolescence, the experiences a teen normally would share with her mother—from learning how to use a sanitary napkin to shopping for a prom dress—must be shared with another family member or negotiated alone. And because a sense of shame often develops around mother loss, a teen will often try to hide or minimize her past. As thirteen-year-old Erika, whose mother died five years ago from amyotrophic lateral sclerosis (Lou Gehrig's disease), explains, "Some people know I don't have a mom and some don't. Her death still bothers me, but usually only when I think about it for a while. I do admit, though, when I see daughters and moms doing things together, I get jealous. I have to do everything with my dad. Sometimes that's a bad thing."

Five to ten years after losing their mothers, most daughters can identify some of the long-term effects—for better and for worse—a mother's illness or absence has had on them. Thirty-three-year-old Judy writes about the close relationship she has with her much-younger sister. Thirty-two-year-old Meredith describes the amazement and sadness she feels when she remembers that the mother she nursed for years will never know her husband or her children. Twenty-eight-year-old Cory worked hard to achieve the dream her mother had for her: she earned a college degree.

Over the past five to ten years, these women have begun to collect the volume and variety of life experiences necessary for them to see how mother loss has shaped, and will continue to shape, their decisions and perspectives. They describe how their grief has evolved over time as their letters repeatedly acknowledge that the acute pain they once felt is no longer a constant in their lives. It's been replaced by a dull longing that is more bearable but, in the words of thirty-three-year-old Judy, "never really goes away."

. . .

## Beth Ann,
*thirty-one, whose mother died of colon cancer seven years ago*

To me, the hardest time to be a motherless daughter was when I lost my first child four years ago. It was the worst possible situation—I was twenty-six weeks along, and was on an overnight business trip three hours from home. I had been feeling fine, but started feeling "sick" in the evening. By the time I decided it was premature labor and my doctor had told me to get to the nearest hospital as soon as possible, I was near panic. Three hours from home, from my doctors, and especially from my husband and father, I *really* needed my mother to talk to. I spent three days in a strange hospital (my husband and father had rushed down that night) while strange doctors worked to stop my premature labor. I kept thinking over and over, "If I could just talk to my mom, maybe I wouldn't be so afraid." After I lost the baby, my dad tried to comfort me, but I really needed my mom there, to have someone who had gone through the same thing tell me why I should want to keep living.

I got pregnant with my daughter just three months later, but I spent my entire pregnancy afraid of every twinge of discomfort. Until my daughter was at least eighteen months old, I checked her several times a night to make sure she was still breathing. I've lost count of the many nights I fell asleep crying, saying to my husband, "If only I could talk to my mom, ask her opinions, find out just how she felt in these situations."

I had a lot of trouble really bonding with my daughter. I was overwhelmed with the responsibility after I had her, and I didn't have my mother around to "compare notes" with. I've tried talking to my mother-in-law, but it's just not the same. I want to be able to just call up my mother and say, "So, how did *you* handle tantrums?"

I've tried talking to others, especially my dad, when I have a question or need advice, but I think I've not really coped all that well. Since my mother's death I've turned to compulsive overeating whenever my emotions overwhelm me. Lately I've begun exercising regularly to reduce some of the stress, but I've still got a long way to go. I'm seeing a therapist for this and related problems.

I don't cry as much anymore, but still hardly a

day goes by that I don't wish I could just talk to her, even one more time.

JUDY,
*thirty-three, whose mother died of pancreatic cancer eight years ago*

We buried my mother, who was forty-six, the day before my twenty-fifth birthday. I have always felt fortunate that I had more years with my mother than do a majority of daughters who lose their moms. My youngest sister was fourteen years old, and my parents were newly divorced at the time of my mother's death. I became the guardian of my younger sister and raised her until she went away to college. The first words she said to me after we returned home from the hospital after our mom died were, "Don't make me go with him," meaning my father. I became a pseudo-mom to my sister, and although it was the most challenging and difficult thing I have done in my life so far, I would do it again.

I still do not have a healthy relationship with my father, who is remarried. I believe my sisters and I get along better with our stepmother than we do with him. The interesting thing about my father is that he carries so much guilt about my mother that I doubt he will ever get past that so he can finally grieve for her. We are constant reminders of her to him, which poses one of the problems that exists between my father and his daughters.

Today I am a mom and have a wonderful son who will be two years old in September. Yes, I expected to have a daughter, but am elated to have a boy. The bond I have with him is strong, and he does fill the void somewhat, as does marriage. But the hole in my heart never really goes away. It amazes me that it has been eight years since my mom left us, and that I still get the same feeling you did when you cried, "I want my mother." It overcomes me without warning. My wedding day and the day I gave birth were probably two of the most emotionally mixed days I have ever experienced. I found that the joy and the sadness have a weird way of mixing together, and what a struggle that is.

One of the only things that hasn't made me insane is that I know my mother is no longer in pain or suffering and is in a much better place. She is always with me, and her voice rings in the back of my head. But oh, what I wouldn't do to have *one second* just to touch her and have her with me for a moment.

SANDY,
*thirty-eight, whose mother died of brain cancer eight and a half years ago*

I lost my mother eight and a half years ago, and sometimes it feels as if it happened only yesterday. My mother was and still is the best friend I ever had. When she was diagnosed with incurable brain cancer, I was thirty years old and the mother of three daughters, ages three, two, and one. I fortunately lived only a couple of miles away and was able to be with my mother constantly. Every morning I took my three girls and went over to spend the day with her. I cleaned, cooked, shopped, helped her shower and go to the bathroom, and read to her. My children made her laugh. I am lucky to have a wonderful husband who did whatever he could to make things better for us all. My two brothers and my sister came by daily to break the monotony. I had the days, and my dad had the nights. He was completely devoted to her. For a year, this was our life. People would ask, "How can you do this to your children?" My answer was, I was doing it *for* my children. They truly learned about love, compassion, and hope.

When my mother died two weeks after her fifty-second birthday, she was in her own home. All her children and my father were around her bed as she quietly slipped away. My daughters had all napped in the same bed with her earlier that day. It was close to midnight, and my father and I wouldn't let them take her to the funeral home until the next morning. We sat by her bed all night, although one of my siblings couldn't bear it and stayed in another room. Daddy and I had been with her every moment of the way, and we weren't willing to let her go yet.

As my father and I sat there talking, I realized that I was still alive. I had truly thought that when my mother died, I would too. It was during that long night that I knew the best thing I could do for my mother was to go on and be the kind of person she always wanted me to be. I have grieved for almost nine years, and always will. There is not a single day that goes by when my mother is not on my mind. My youngest daughter is named after her; my house holds her things; she is in my soul; my mother is me.

The day after my mother died, I noticed a piece of paper on top of a box in her closet. It was something she had written to herself in 1972 after losing her father, who had also died of brain cancer. This letter has brought me and many other people I have given it to great comfort. It sits in a frame on my desk, and I read it every day:

> Who said my father is gone? He is here—
> I see him—I smell him. I touch him.
> Who said I lost my father?

Who said my father is dead—who said it? How can he be dead—We're all here—my mother, my sisters and brother, my children, my nieces and nephews.

When you're dead there is nothing—but there is something—I feel the lump in my throat—My head hurts—I have his sweater— with some of his hair on it. I have his chair. I have his deck of cards that he held in his hands. I smell my father—I want him. I won't give him up. Who said I lost my father?

Last year I lost a very good friend at the age of thirty-eight to breast cancer. She had struggled for five years. Adele left behind two daughters, seven and four years old. The cancer had been discovered when she was pregnant with her second. We became close only after she got sick. Adele was able to confide her true feelings to me because she knew if I could handle my mother's death I could handle anything.

Today, I have a wonderful life. My husband is the best, and my girls are healthy, happy, and beautiful. I live in a very strong, supportive community. I have friends that have been there for me for years, and a full life. I help my husband run our business and am active in many organizations. Because of my mother, I do the very best I can for those around me.

I could go on and on. I know that we share the

same bond, a bond that can only be shared by daughters who have lost their mothers. Just writing this letter has made me feel better. Reading your words, you reading mine, I know we are friends.

Our lives have all been touched, for good and bad. The pain will never go away, but we do go on.

## CORY,

*twenty-eight, whose mother died of cervical cancer nine years ago*

My mother died when she was forty-three and I was nineteen. To this day, I continue to miss her. My mother was a poor, uneducated single parent living in a low-income housing project. We survived on state assistance and received medical care at rural clinics.

I am the youngest of her five children. As my mother was dying, I was struggling to care for her full-time and attend the local city college on limited funds. She chose to die at home, in the projects, with the care of her children. I went from seeing an active, proud mother to seeing a helpless, weak young woman who had had a hard life but who continued to be extremely proud of her children's accomplishments.

Today, I'm married with no children. I was educated at a state university, and received a B.A. degree in social work. I work in the child-protection field. The loss of my mother and the loss of my father just two months ago have left me feeling empty and yet proud of what I come from. I think the drive to get an education and be successful that my mother instilled in her children is what keeps me strong and invested in women's issues.

I believe women and mothers are the core of a nurturing family and planet. Politically speaking, if more mothers were world leaders, we'd see less war and poverty.

LYNN,

*twenty-six, whose mother died of breast cancer nine years ago*

My mother died when I was seventeen. She was a single parent, and I was an only child. We lived alone.

My mother was the driving force behind my success as a child. I excelled in academics, and from the sixth grade to the twelfth grade I had full scholarships at the most prestigious private schools in the state. I was a very good dancer and actress—at age fourteen, I was an apprentice with the state ballet. I was pretty, smart, and talented, and my mother and grandmother were very proud of me.

I have never felt as pretty or smart or talented as I was as a child. It took me five and a half years to complete college with a barely average grade point average. Instead of being a theater major and dealing with the heavy competition, I took an easier way out. I did a lot of drugs and was promiscuous. In other words, without my mother pushing me along, I really had no idea how to push myself, how to praise myself, how to be myself.

I guess I've spent a lot of time feeling like my mother was the foundation to my success, and when she died, my foundation was pulled out from beneath me. I've been living on some very shaky ground. I've only very recently been learning how to build my own solid foundation. It's very difficult because not only am I a motherless daughter, but I'm also fatherless, grandmotherless, and sister/brotherless.

In the past, people have described me as very defensive. But now I think my emotions have leveled out, and I'm no longer in so much denial about everything. So I'm coping much better—most of the time.

## MEREDITH,

*thirty-two, whose mother died of cancer ten years ago*

One week ago was the ten-year anniversary of my mother's death. It happened two days after my twenty-second birthday. (To this day, I believe she held out for those two days so she wouldn't die on or so close to my birthday.) I am thirty-two now, and finally realize I have a loss and a pain that will never leave me. (So it only took me ten years to realize this; okay, I'm a bit slow.) I cared for my mother for nineteen months with very little support from the rest of my family. To tell you that it was a very difficult time doesn't really come close to what it was like.

The memories that I have not let myself remember for a long time came flooding back to me as I read your book. The day my mother went to take a shower after being in the hospital for more than a week, it was all she talked about. What we didn't realize was that she was too weak to have one alone until she stood there naked and shivering in the bathroom, her body resembling an ad for Care. Her eyes filled with tears. She looked like a child would look to an adult, silently pleading for me to help her. Without thinking, I jumped into the shower, fully clothed, and held her arms for support. She started to wash, and then, realizing what I had done, she began to laugh. We were laughing so hard that my father knocked on the door asking if we were all right, which only made us laugh harder.

There was the day I went into her hospital room and she handed me her hairbrush and asked me to help her. She couldn't stand the fact that every time she moved her head, clumps of hair would fall out. I brushed and brushed, hiding my horror as her beautiful, dark hair fell into my hands. She didn't cry, not one tear. When I finished, a bald woman thanked me and said, "There, that's done."

I held my mother's hand when she died. My sister and both of our best friends were also in the room. I watched her last breath, still unsure as I asked my sister, "Is she . . . ?" "Yes," my sister whispered. I immediately looked up to the ceiling, expecting to see her soul. Later as I sat alone with her body, I studied her fingers and hands. She had the most beautiful hands.

A few months after my mother died, I had been out one night with a boy I dated before my mother got sick. We went to the beach to see the sunrise. I came home to find my father sitting at our dining room table with his head in his hands, crying. This was the first time I had ever seen my father cry. Panic seized me: I thought someone else had died. I was shocked when he told me he was worried because he didn't know where I was. When I was growing up, my father was very much the absent

father. As he was organizing the first peace movement march in our town during the Vietnam War,
my mother was teaching me to swim, driving me to
tennis lessons, and listening to the problems a ten-
year-old has. My mother set curfews, as well as the
other rules in our house. After my mother died, it
never, not once, occurred to me to let my dad know
where I was when I went out. So here sat my father,
basically a stranger to me, crying and telling me,
"Meredith, I just don't know how it works." I explained that before Mom had gotten sick, she and I
had a very trusting relationship, and I would call her
if I was going to be out past midnight. I would tell
her where I was and who I was with. She'd let me
know if she was comfortable with that. She knew my
friends, and it was almost never a problem. Even
then, my dad could not set rules on his own. He
asked me in disbelief, "You call at midnight? You
don't come home then?" (This man was my father
for twenty-two years; how could he not have known
this?)

My father was devastated when a few months
later I told him I would be moving to the Midwest.
He never understood that I moved across the United
States to leave the role of caretaker that my family
immediately gave me, the youngest child. I have two
older brothers and one sister, who were all grown
and out of the house when I was growing up. Each
one has his/her own demons and was unable to cope

with my mother's illness. Out of the three, only my sister and I have any contact. There was a lot of damage done during those years my mother was ill. My sister resented the fact that I was able to cope, and I still cannot forgive her that she couldn't. When I was little, I idolized my sister. So the devastation I felt when she abandoned my mother and myself was immense. When she finally had the courage to come around, the damage had been done. My mother had grown unbelievably dependent on me. I remember when my sister went to help my mother one day and my mother said, "No, we must ask Meredith . . . she knows how to." I will never forget the hatred in my sister's eyes. To this day, it is there between us.

In the nineteen months my mother lived with cancer, I had five days off. I flew to Chicago to see a good friend. We went to a club, and I danced with a college student I met. I told him everything he wanted to know about me except for one small detail: that I took care of my mother, who was dying from cancer. I let him believe I was nothing other than a twenty-two-year-old visiting her friend. The depression was so severe when I had to leave, I didn't think I would be physically able to get on the plane. (Maybe it was the look my mother acquired in her eyes that I could no longer bear. She had been cheated out of her life, and she knew it. As each month passed, a bit of my mother slipped away till I hardly recognized the woman I was caring for.)

When I got home, my mother had left little notes on my bed welcoming me back and telling me funny little details that went on while I was gone. She came to the door of my room, wanting to hear all about my trip. I didn't even hug her. I rushed past her and was sick in our bathroom. I was so upset and angry at the fact that I wasn't that girl I pretended to be on my trip. I was a young girl who had come home to watch her mother deteriorate in front of her eyes. All of my friends had gone off to universities and had their whole lives to look forward to. I had nothing to look forward to but watching my mother die. But worse was the cold treatment I had toward her that day. She was hurt by it, and I couldn't stop. I was as bad as my sister, who had deserted her in the beginning; it just took me a little longer. This memory still haunts me. If I was granted any day in my entire life to relive, it would be that day.

After quite a few painful relationships, I met the man I knew I would marry five years ago. We were married last summer. It still seems unreal to me that my mother never got to meet him. I have no doubt in my mind they would have quickly become friends. It amazes me, that this is the man I plan to spend the rest of my life with and he has never heard my mother's laughter or seen the sparkle in her eyes when her sense of humor was at its best. I alternate between disbelief that she is not here to see my life as an adult and anger that I have been cheated out of hearing her say to me, "What a great guy he is. You sure had me worried, kiddo, with all those years of surfers coming through the door. And you marry a European—who would have thought!"

A wonderful woman I met years ago while caring for my grandmother told me that no one would ever love me like my mother did. It still brings tears to my eyes when I remember her telling me this. This quest I have been on to fill the void has brought up three older women in my life who are my surrogate mothers. Each one reminds me of my own mother in one way or another. The woman I have known the longest and am closest to was my "mother for the day" on my wedding day. Just before I was to walk into the church, she hugged me and whispered, "Your mother is right here beside you, you sweet child. Don't think she isn't." I firmly believe this—that my mother is beside me and inside me and always will be. I refuse to forget her. Maybe the sound of her voice has faded from my memory, but the love she gave me, the sense of humor she passed on to me, and the sense of integrity that she possessed are here waiting for me to pass on to my child, when I find the courage to have one.

When I was eighteen, I moved away from home. My mom gave me a travel alarm clock with a card that is now framed and in my bathroom. I read it each morning. "To Meredith, to wish you the best of time in the future, to keep you on time for all of your appointments, and to remind you that I love you all of the time. Mother." I know my mother and I would have been friends if she had lived. I know that she would be proud of me at times and disappointed in me as well. (With all my travels and adventures, going to a university was not one of them. To this day, wherever she is, I'll bet that bothers her.) But I also know she would love me unconditionally, like only a mother can, like only my mother did.

*Chapter Three*

## ON THE OUTSIDE LOOKING IN: TEN TO TWENTY YEARS

By the time ten years have elapsed since a mother's death, most daughters have shifted their focus away from the actual death or departure and toward the impact the loss has had on them. As they identify mother loss as a pivotal event—perhaps *the* pivotal event—of their lives thus far, they may begin to view it as the logical explanation for all that has happened to them since. For some daughters, this is accurate: a mother's death very well may have set off a chain of challenging or adverse events that still resonates today. Other daughters, however, may rely on a mother's death as a plausible and convenient explanation for any negative adult experiences. The child who felt helpless when her mother died must resist growing into an adult who uses that death as an excuse for not taking control of her own life.

As the daughters in this chapter move through

the adult transitions and decisions of their twenties and thirties, they mourn the loss of support and advice they believe their mothers would have provided. The daughter without a mother tends to romanticize and idealize the potential of her lost relationship, often envisioning her mother's presence as a cure-all for her current woes. These women must acknowledge that while many living mothers do offer guidance to adult daughters, many others do not. At this point, it becomes necessary for a motherless woman to work on humanizing her lost mother, to gather as much information as she can about her, and to accept both the positive and the negative points about her as a woman and as a mother.

One of the motherless woman's most challenging long-term tasks of mourning is to develop a realistic picture of her mother, to adopt the qualities she admires, and to reject the rest. All daughters must do this to some degree, but the daughter with a living mother has accessible images—both Good Mother and Bad Mother—she can accept and reject. The daughter who's lost her mother has to piece together her image through memory and investigative research. When the mother has been idealized or sanctified, which frequently happens after a loved one dies, the daughter has no Bad Mother to resist. When she focuses only on her mother's good traits, she creates an unrealistic and impossible standard for herself to achieve.

In this chapter, we see daughters who lost their mothers between ten and twenty years ago searching for ways to keep the memory of the Good Mother, as well as their connections to her, alive. Twenty-nine-year-old Maggie, who lost her mother eleven years ago, writes about the "ongoing conversations" they continue to have. Thirty-four-year-old Phoebe, whose mother died fourteen years ago, has done genealogical research on her mother's family, trying to develop and maintain a connection to all her maternal relatives.

In this chapter we also read women's accounts of what psychologists call "arrested development." This occurs when parts of a child's emotional development freeze at the time of a childhood trauma such as mother loss. Some daughters describe feeling as if their personalities have split—they can go through the motions of their peer group, yet still feel like children. As twenty-three-year-old Robbie, who was five when her mother died of cancer, explains:

> On the one hand, I'm a very responsible and mature person for my age. I have a full-time job and am a full-time student. I've been working and studying full-time for four years. A lot of people I know tell me that I'm the oldest young person they know, which I find

funny but ironic. The irony is in the fact that so often I feel as though I'm still a little girl, still five years old, very scared and shy and without a mother, always a little lost and feeling as though I'm on the outside looking in.

At the same time that women like Robbie identify long-term difficulties they attribute to early mother loss, they also write of their strong sense of resilience and self-pride. These daughters have experienced the most traumatic loss a young child can imagine, and have survived. Armed with this knowledge, many motherless women believe they can face virtually any adverse event in the future, and persevere.

. . .

MAGGIE,
*twenty-nine, whose mother died of cancer eleven years ago*

My mother died when I was eighteen, and I had not really begun to give deep thought to her death's effect on me until I read your book. You spoke and wrote about the continuing conversations that motherless daughters have with their mothers long after their death. This does not necessarily mean talking to an image, but is usually a search for an answer to,

"What would she have liked me to do?" There are two "conversations" I've had with my mother that stand out and that I'd like to share with you.

The first came right after my mother passed away, and I was given the task of deciding what clothes to forward to the funeral home to dress her in for burial. The responsibility fell on my shoulders, as I was the younger sister of two older brothers and thus was the only female left in the immediate family. I had, of course, no experience in picking out clothes for interment. What does one choose? The most comfortable and attractive clothing for the hereafter? Would my mother's ghost be forever regretting the outfit I chose for her? I decided that she would've killed me if I buried anything good. I could hear her saying, "Of all things, why would you put a Perry Ellis blazer in a coffin for eternity? You could still get good use from it." I then thought I'd pick a dress that she'd worn at one of the happier times in her life. She had lived with cancer for six years prior to her death, so it would have to have been before the time she became sick. I chose the dress she wore on the day of my brother's graduation. It was a typical midseventies dress, so it wasn't "too good" for burial, but she'd worn it at a happy occasion—the accomplishment of one of her children. No one questioned my choice. I still don't know why. When I look back at this now, I can't believe the thought that went into this decision, particularly for an eighteen-year-old. But, then again, she helped me make the decision.

A second ongoing conversation I still have is whether or not to visit her grave. The only time after the funeral that I have been there was a year after her death. One of the positive results of my mother's death is a profound appreciation for those people who are still here. As a result, my focus that day at her grave was on how nice it was to be holding my father's arm and looking at the blank space next to my mother's name on the headstone.

I have not been back to her grave since. I feel that it wouldn't do much good to remember my mother by staring at her grave. If I want to visit her spirit, I am much better off going clothes shopping at Loehmann's. We shared many wonderful times there that could only be shared with a daughter. Loehmann's was also the place where she went for "therapy." For now, I've decided that visiting my mother's grave is not something she would have wanted me to do. She would have preferred that I carry out her spirit by living an independent, happy life, as she taught me to do by words and example. I can remember her or speak to her anywhere, and often do.

Some women who've lost their mothers say they needed to see their mothers' bodies after death, to say a proper good-bye. I never wanted to see my mother without life. As I mentioned, I'd lived with my mother and her cancer for six years before she died. I'd learned to express my love for her whenever I felt it. I didn't need to see my mother's body for closure. I didn't want to have a memory of what she looked like after death. She hadn't, in fact, looked like herself for some time. The disease and her medication had altered her appearance. In the last month of her life, the surgery on her brain, where the cancer had finally spread after beginning in her breast, had almost completely taken away her ability to communicate. So, just as I'd chosen not to helplessly ride behind the ambulance taking her to the hospital, or enter her hospital room after she died, or see her in her coffin, I chose instead to live with the memories of my mother full of life, and not without it.

## DEENA,

*twenty-six, whose mother committed suicide twelve years ago*

My friend Elaine told me about your book. Elaine's mother died of cancer, and she said I should read it. So I did. I'm a survivor, too. My mother suicided when I turned fourteen. She was forty-three. She may have benefited from your book, since she had lost her mother to suicide at a young age. My grandmother also was forty-three when she died. Mommy was fourteen at the time. I guess she never really got over it, worked through it, or accepted it. Those twenty-nine years in between were somewhat of a living hell for her. Or so I imagine.

I've been writing in a journal for years and it isn't always easy. But it's the best gift I could have given myself—the gift of sanity. No, I'm not depressed or suicidal or unhappy, but you just reaffirmed for me that all of us "mother-challenged" (if you're into political correctness, which I am *not*) girls go through this. Or parts of it. And we make it just fine. Some of us actually lead normal lives . . . but we do feel that, to a certain degree, we *are* different.

My friend Elaine and I got to know each other shortly after I moved to the Midwest for my job. She showed up at my firm. Slim and beautiful, she walked past our receptionist, who commented on how thin she was getting. I asked Nina if she could tell me the secret to Elaine's slimness, and Nina said that her mother had been diagnosed with cancer, and that's why Elaine moved back to town, to spend whatever time her mother had left with her.

I had never met Elaine, but I sent her a note letting her know that I had lost my mother and that I could probably relate—and that I could certainly provide two ears and two shoulders. A few days later, Elaine and I went to lunch, cried over a Caesar salad, and became friends. That was two years ago, and I don't think we'll ever lose touch, even though I now live more than five hundred miles away.

Since I'm only twenty-six, I still have seventeen years to get to that "fated" forty-three. It's a year, I'm sure, which will be pretty uneventful for me, since the biggest lesson I learned from a grandmother I never met and a mother I forgave is that life, this life, *my life*, is tremendously fun and worth living.

## PHOEBE,
*thirty-four, whose mother died in an accident fourteen years ago*

My mother was killed by a drunk driver when she was forty-nine years old. My brother, age thirteen at the time, was with her and was nearly killed, but survived with no long-term *physical* problems. My parents had been married nearly twenty-two years. I had been living away from home for about three years and was married with a fourteen-month-old baby boy.

I was very close to my mother. We talked nearly every day and saw each other weekly (we lived a little over an hour apart). My father, on the other hand, was very emotionally distant and withholding. Nothing was ever good enough for him. He had a short temper, but was not what you would call phys-ically abusive. He was in the military for more than twenty years, so we moved quite a bit while I was growing up.

I honestly couldn't tell you how I've gotten through life to this point with my sanity intact with everything that happened concerning my mother's death and the chain of events I believe it spawned. What basically happened after my mother died is as follows: I got involved with an old boyfriend; I was divorced from my first husband; got pregnant with my second child by the old boyfriend; lost custody of my son to my first husband's mother, who lives in another state; moved back home with my father; had another baby boy; not long after my son was born, married someone I barely knew who was physically and mentally abusive; and divorced after a year. I moved back in with my dad and started school; moved in with a man I met there and then married him within a year; finished school; got a good job but quit after three years to move to the Virgin Is-lands when my husband got a job transfer; lost ev-erything I owned in Hurricane Hugo; my husband had an affair (he still lives with the woman now); my father died from prostate cancer, leaving all his money to the National Wildlife Federation (money from the lawsuit related to my mother's death, part of which my brother and I were supposed to have received in the first place). At about that time, I moved back to the United States; went back to my old job; lost more than sixty pounds in less than three months and started a borderline eating disorder; divorced again; was involved with an abusive, crazy man; got pregnant and had an abortion; got away from him; and lost one of my best friends, my "almost second mother" who took me in after my father died and helped me get back on my feet in the States. After dating many, many men, I finally met the most perfect person for me, someone who is very good to me and whom I love and respect more than anyone. Now I'm happy, but I still miss and need my mother. I still think of her every day.

I was able to type out this nice, long list of events, which doesn't give any weight to their significance, but they were all major, life-altering events that severely disrupted my life. I feel like I was caught in some kind of whirlwind, completely out of control.

I am not proud of these events, most of which I brought on myself. It hasn't been until the past couple of years that I realized a lot of this had to do with my mother's death. What bothers me the most, and what I hesitate to tell people for fear of what they'll think of me, is the serial marriages and relationships and, most importantly, losing custody of my son. I'm considered an intelligent, stable, mature, dependable, responsible person who is not difficult to get along with, and not the type of person to have had all this happen to! It seems to me that all this boils down to having an emotionally distant father and to losing my mother so young. These two things have created such an emptiness I was always trying to fill through relationships, and pain I was always trying to numb. All my marriages occurred within a five-year period following my mother's death—by the time I was twenty-three I had been married three times!

My brother is even worse off. As a teenager, he got involved with drugs and alcohol and dropped out of school. My father sent him to a residential drug rehab center when he was fifteen or sixteen and told him if he ever used drugs again, he would be kicked out of the house. He was kicked out the next year and has been on his own ever since, living with me a couple of times. Just after the "accident" he told me that he felt it was his fault because he had talked my mother into staying at his karate studio, where they were on their way home from. No one in the family ever blamed him or said it was his fault, but he denies having said this now. He goes from menial job to menial job, place to place, and person to person. He has always had a drinking problem and has had some DUIs—even with his mother having been killed by a drunk driver and himself almost killed! I have tried to help him on more than one occasion, but he only takes advantage of me and lies and steals from me. Although we live in the same city, I never hear from him unless he wants something. He has learned that I won't loan him money anymore, so I don't hear from him very often. My son adores him and we feel like he's the only family we have now, but we don't really have him at all.

My son never knew his grandmother and is saddened by this. He loves for me to tell him stories about her, and he seems to love this woman he has never known. I had a horrible adolescence, and my mother and I were just beginning the adult phase of our relationship. I felt as if I had almost "made up" to her for all the trouble and pain I had caused her, and then she was taken away from me. There is still so much I would like to know, talks I'd like to have, things to share and do together. At the same time, I'm glad she didn't have to grow old and ill or suffer from a long and painful illness, and I'm glad she wasn't around to see my father go through his illness or to have to live without him after his death.

I am definitely independent and extremely strong and resilient. People often tell me they are amazed that I have been through so much and not only am alive and sane but also am a very optimistic, upbeat person. I have not allowed any of the bad experiences in my life to make me bitter or bring me down. I have always ended up better off after each adversity. At the same time, I still feel like an afraid little girl who needs to be loved and taken care of. I don't want to be a martyr and hope I don't come across sounding like one. I only want people to understand and to accept and love me as I am. I believe I've found that person, but I have such a high regard for him that I feel "flawed" and as if I have to constantly explain everything so I'll feel he'll understand. This all comes from myself; he doesn't do anything to make me feel this way. Men in the past have said they felt as if they couldn't live up to my high standards and expectations.

In your chapter titled "Mortal Lessons" you write about women fearing they will die of the same disease their mothers did. Sometimes I do fear dying in a car accident or some other tragic way, but I also fear not knowing what diseases I may be predisposed to. I don't know if my mother would have acquired breast cancer, some other form of cancer, heart disease, or any other number of diseases. She had smoked since she was a teenager and never wanted to quit. Actually, now I'm kind of glad she didn't, since as it turns out, it wasn't necessary for her health. Her older sister, however, did die of lung cancer two years after my mother's death. Yet I still smoke! I know it's stupid, and I always thought it was because I was highly addicted and just didn't want to quit. After reading your book, I wonder if it isn't part of the "risk taking" you wrote about or a feeling that I'm going to die some tragic death at a young age, so there's no need to quit. Or perhaps

I'm just testing the limits of my own mortality—I don't know about this one!

One thing I've done to stay close to my mother and to find out more about her is genealogy research. Several years after her death I began researching my extended family history on my mother's side. I didn't grow up around my extended family, and I barely even knew my grandparents. I still work on this research to this day.

## BETTY,

*thirty-nine, whose mother died of cancer thirteen years ago*

My mother died about one month after yours. She was just fifty-three years old. She, too, had cancer (three types of leukemia, including a childhood type). Her pain from the disease was misdiagnosed as a "sprained leg" by an indifferent doctor. What she had was phlebitis *with* the leukemias. She entered the hospital for chemo five months before she died.

She was a valiant fighter. She used to tell me that even though she felt the doctors used her like a guinea pig (she had five rounds of different chemotherapies in less than six months' time), she hoped what she suffered would help someone else live.

Unfortunately, because of his own emotional dysfunction, my father made the choice to leave my mother in the hospital to die, even though Mum wanted to be at home. I was in my late twenties—the oldest of five children, all born within seven years' span—and refused to believe that my father's unilateral decision was the final word. My younger sister, my then-husband, and I set up a meeting with the hospital doctor to discuss the practicality of letting my mother go home. When the doctor walked in and discovered that my father was not part of the meeting, he refused to talk with us and walked out of the room!

My mother died sometime after Johnny Carson's monologue (she rarely missed his opening monologue!), all alone, in reverse isolation in the oncology ward. Those are still bitter memories . . .

I've been through the grief stages and through counseling, but the times I will miss my mother the most are, I know, yet to come.

My first husband was abusive. My mother knew, at least as much as I dared let anyone know at that time. We divorced about five years ago. Now I am a newlywed, wanting a family, wanting my wonderful new husband to know my mother, wanting her to know him, wanting my mother to be Grandma to my children . . . the list never seems to end. I want my mother to rejoice with me in my new life and love, but . . . she's not here.

I, too, have experienced the unthinking cruelty in the remarks of those who have mothers and just do *not* understand. I know the sick feeling and little-girl shame that sometimes comes from the well-meaning, cheery "encouragement" to get on with my life . . . or the reminder that it's been "years since she died" (unspoken: Why does it still bother you?).

I think another factor in my grief and pain was that my father never dealt with his loss. He immediately began to date the mother of my brother's then-fiancé. (He hardly knew her, and pushed my mother for an introduction.) In less than five months after my mother died, my brother's engagement broke off and, instead, my father married the ex-fiancé's mother. It's hard to grieve healthily when your mother's place is already "filled."

Subsequent losses hurt so much more now that my mother is no longer here. I am glad we became good friends before her illness and death, but then, there are all those shared moments that are now missed. No matter who the other person is, it's not the same as a moment with Mum.

## LAUREN,

*thirty-seven, whose mother died of heart disease fourteen years ago*

I'm the mother of a six-year-old son, and in the process of getting a divorce. My mother died when I was twenty-three, of an unexpected, degenerative heart disease at age fifty-four.

I was very close to her. She was my biggest supporter and fan. We really enjoyed each other, staying up late into the night talking, smoking cigarettes, and drinking water. We read the same books, and she was intelligent and open-minded.

For a number of years, probably ten, I just couldn't deal with her death. In my family, we never even mentioned her name for years because it upset my dad so much. Because it hurt too much to feel, I just numbed out that part of me. I tried to compensate by compulsive overeating and smoking (until three years ago), getting overinvolved in other people's lives trying to re-create that security, and mothering others.

Perhaps my mother's death elevated what her importance in my life was to be. If she were alive, she may not have been that big of an influence, but the loss of her prevents me from knowing that for sure. To me, she was my biggest supporter and I lost that. I lost that person who thought I was the greatest, no matter what.

I know if my mother were alive we would fight, she would make me mad, shame me—the usual irritating things mothers do. She would also love me, listen to me, support me emotionally, cook for me, care for me, mother me. I could have somewhere to go home to where I didn't always have to be in charge and "on." I still miss my mom with tears in my eyes when I let myself think about her.

## SHELLY,
*thirty-two, whose mother died of cancer fifteen years ago*

I was seventeen when my mother died, the youngest of seven children and the only one still at home. My father was incapable of helping me deal with the loss ("don't feel bad" was his most common phrase). To learn that many others have suffered long-lasting effects from similar situations is startling and very helpful.

By twenty-five, I was finally getting through the days without grieving. Two primary aspects of my particular experience have since become clear and have helped me to understand and accept my life more fully.

First, I had not separated emotionally from my

mother at seventeen, like many teenagers do, which made her death more earth-shattering for me. I've wondered long and hard *why* she was my only emotional support, and why our mutual passion for the arts has left me perpetually searching for her replacement so I can again share my interests with someone as fully.

Counseling since the age of twenty-seven has helped me to understand the other piece of the puzzle, which in turn helps to explain the first piece: since early childhood I have experienced a deep-seated and traumatic fear of my older siblings. As a precocious and emotionally needy and vulnerable child, I was the main target of intersibling conflicts. My father was emotionally unavailable for the kids, and my mother had trouble managing all the emotional demands of seven children. Thus, I had many "walls" up to try and protect myself emotionally, and Mother was my only line of defense in the house. What I have gained more than anything from reading your book is the terribly important realization that there wasn't anything basically wrong with me because I had not separated emotionally from my mother. In my situation, it would have been too threatening to my emotional security to do so. I believe my mother had an anxious awareness of what was in store for me, but her decline from cancer was so rapid (fifteen weeks total) that she had no time to help or to try to rectify some of the family's emotional dysfunctions.

A physical side-effect of the two facets of my family experience, particularly since my mother's death, has been chronic physical tension in my breathing (my abdomen) and my upper back. It is highly coincidental that I received your book the same week I was concluding ten sessions of a holistic treatment called "Rolfing" that has literally made me taller by straightening my posture and releasing major, chronic deposits of tension in the musculature of my body. So, along with the miracle of understanding more about my life, I am experiencing a sense of physical ease and relaxation that I haven't known for at least fifteen years. I think that the coincidence was of her planning . . .

Somehow, since Mother's death, I've experienced a strong and clear belief that there is life beyond death and that she is there. I also am truly not afraid of dying—only of experiencing pain in an accidental or illness-related death. This is because I know that she will be there waiting for me wherever I go, and I will experience the bliss of communicating directly with her again. Her death somehow inexplicably brought me this gift. In the past year, I've also started volunteer work with hospice, which is one way I can perhaps help those who are dealing with the fear of death.

## ROBBIE,

*twenty-three, whose mother died of cancer eighteen years ago*

I am the youngest child in a family of six children, five girls and one boy. My mother died when I was five years old of cancer that began in her throat and spread way too quickly throughout her body. She was a beautiful, gentle woman who died seven months before her forty-second birthday. My sisters were nineteen, sixteen, thirteen, and eight years old. I am still grieving over my mother, and I feel as though it is a process I will be going through for the rest of my life.

One of the most difficult aspects for me is that I have no recollection of any of the five years prior to my mother's death, or the next two to three years after, and then I can remember only bits and pieces. I wonder if that period of time will ever come back to me at all in some form or if it is completely lost in some mental repression chasm that I cannot quite reach. I have always thought my sisters were lucky because they remember Mom, whereas I can't really remember her at all. Yet I miss her so much. I can't tell you how many times I've thought, "If only she were here, this wouldn't be happening." Some days I miss her so very much that I ache and I can't stop the tears.

I have a theory that some people think is a little strange, so I usually don't tell anyone, but I wanted to share it with you. I wonder if other motherless daughters do this as well. When I pray, I pray to my mother as well as to God. The reason for this is because I honestly feel as though my mother is my guardian angel. Throughout my life I have been in many situations that were bad for me or life-threatening, from having unprotected sex when I was younger with chances of pregnancy and/or diseases or AIDS to car accidents to police situations. Yet I have been fortunate in that I have always come through okay. Despite being in such situations, I am all right and my life is the way it should be, at least according to me. Even when something bad has happened, I feel it is my mom trying to teach me a lesson somehow, to turn me in another direction before it gets worse. Maybe because she wasn't able to stay in my world long enough to teach and tell me some things herself, this is how she compensates.

I was lucky that I had the rest of my family. I consider myself raised by my father and my sisters, who all gave me very much love and caring. My father remarried a year after my mother's death, and my sisters really had a hard time with that. None of them really have a good relationship with my stepmother, who had two children of her own, making us eight. She doesn't help the situation either. She resents all of us a great deal, probably because we are living proof that my father actually loved someone else and had a life before her. I know she has had a hard time with me simply because I look just like my mother, and according to everyone in my family who knew her, even have her personality. My father tells me that God took her but left him me. I don't take this negatively, though. As a matter of fact, I take this as a very special compliment.

## LIESL,

*thirty-eight, whose mother died of cancer sixteen years ago*

I was almost twenty-three when my mother died. She was fifty-eight. Like you, I was just beginning my journey as an adult. And also like you, I often have a sense of "being stuck" at that stage of my development, that I've not emotionally matured past twenty-three years of age.

How has the loss of my mother at a young age impacted my growth? How could I have come so successfully into adulthood in spite of it? I have everything and more than she had wished for me: a career; a loving, happy family of my own; good friends. Still, there is a vacant place within my soul that I persist in maintaining for her. It is sixteen years later, and she is still missed at the Thanksgiving table. She was missed at my daughter's birth, first words, first steps. She is the person I want to phone after my husband and I have had a tiff. But I think her absence is felt most at ordinary moments, like when I'm shopping for baby clothes, tending my garden, driving down a beautiful stretch of road— and listening to my friends "complain" about their own, still-living mothers. So many times I want to chide others for the way they take their mothers for granted. And just as often, I feel real envy for their ability to pick up the phone and share a chat with Mom.

Only a few days after my mother died, I dialed her number just to hear it ring, to fantasize she was out of the house on an errand. In a way, I think I am still doing this mentally, and probably will continue. It's my way of keeping her alive, and of keeping her with me.

# Chapter Four

# EXPERIENCE TURNS TO INSIGHT: TWENTY TO THIRTY YEARS

Having lived through more than two decades since the loss of their mothers, the daughters in this chapter show evidence of deeper levels of reflection and awareness. They've had enough time not only to think about the long-term effects of mother loss, but also to actually see how that early event has influenced the course of their lives. Their stories are longer and more richly developed, more retrospectives than letters.

Although a woman whose mother died twenty-five years ago may still think of her every day, her periods of deep longing are usually triggered by very specific joyful or painful events. Even so, these daughters may find themselves surprised by the intensity of their grief at those times. Subsequent losses in particular, such as a father's death or the loss of a job, may send a daughter back to mourn another piece of her earlier loss, and can evoke in her the same emotions and fears she had when her mother died. It's important for these women to remember that mourning can only be resolved *to the best of a daughter's ability at any particular time in her life.* That's why the daughter who feels she's worked through her grief for her mother at age thirty, for example, may find herself facing additional challenges at thirty-eight that send her back to rework the loss from her slightly altered perspective.

By now, a significant transformation has typically occurred: the daughter's longing for *her* mother, who continues to recede further into the past, has been replaced by a more generalized longing for *a* mother. When we use the word *Mother*, we're not always referring to a specific person, but often to a set of behaviors we associate with a maternal figure: security, support, comfort, nurturing. Adult motherless women haven't lost the need or the desire for such a figure in their lives. By their thirties and forties, however, many have become aware of their tendency to project their need for a mother onto their relationships with others. Forty-three-year-old Marlene writes about the disappointments she encountered when she expected her husband and her in-laws to fill that role. Thirty-three-year-old Joanne writes of her reluctance to enjoy intimacy with her young daughter, for fear that she will try to extract the love from her daughter that she imagines she'd get from a mother.

Several daughters in this chapter are approaching or have already reached the "Magic Number," the age a mother was when she died. Unlike most of their peers, who must live into their seventies or eighties to exceed their mothers' final ages, most women who lost their mothers young reach this transitional time in middle age.

Motherless women who are approaching the Magic Number often feel a powerful urge to live a full life, with no excuses and no regrets. Explains forty-year-old Laura, whose mother died twenty years ago at the age of fifty-four:

> I live with the fear that my life will be cut short, as my mother's was. I have the desire to cram in as much as I can before reaching age fifty—the year of my mother's cancer diagnosis and mastectomy. So what do I do? Scuba dive, sky dive, white-water raft, ski, travel . . . People think that I have a death wish. They just don't understand that if I don't meet certain challenges *now*, there might not be enough time to experience the thrill of these activities *later*.

Reaching the Magic Number often triggers a grief response in a motherless woman. It's a time of both sadness and rebirth. The daughter fears leaving her mother behind—and may feel guilty for seeing years her mother never got to see—but also feels relieved that her destiny will differ from her mother's. Forty-year-old Gayle, whose mother died twenty-seven years ago at the age of thirty-six, says her own thirty-seventh birthday was "spooky." All day long, she recalls, she kept hearing the *Twilight Zone* theme song playing in her head.

Women who have children often find themselves having a similar response when their first child reaches the age they were when their mothers died. For the first time they understand as adults, they explain, how much a child of that age understands and feels, and they can see how much that child still needs a mother.

The causes of loss that appear in this chapter are varied, ranging from long-term illness to sudden, accidental death. Twenty to thirty years after their mothers have died, the women whose letters follow repeatedly show how, over time, the specific cause of death profoundly affects the daughters left behind. Thirty-six-year-old Janet, whose mother died in a plane crash, learned at the age of twelve that death can arrive at any moment and has developed what she describes as a morbid preoccupation with trying to evade it. Thirty-six-year-old Barbara, whose mother died of a stroke twenty-three years ago, is "militantly anti-diet" today because she believes that her mother's eating habits contributed to her death. And thirty-seven-year-old Lois, whose mother died of colon cancer twenty-six years ago, has struggled ever since with her fear of developing cancer.

Thirty-year-old Adora, who suffered from undetected abuse within her nuclear family after her mother died, shows us how a family's coping methods can create additional trauma for a young girl. Her story and others in this chapter serve as reminders that as the years pass, the age at which a mother died and the family's response to the death may have as profound an impact on a daughter as the actual loss itself.

• • •

## LAURA,

*forty, whose mother died of breast cancer twenty years ago*

Twenty years after my mother's death, I still have her seal coat in my closet. Sure, I've thought about restyling it through the years, but just never got around to it. I guess subconsciously it was just comforting to know that a part of my mother was close by. I think it's about time that someone a bit more needy should benefit from its warmth.

My mother died in August 1974 at age fifty-four from breast cancer. I was twenty years old (three weeks shy of my twenty-first birthday) and just two weeks away from returning to college to complete my senior year. I not only lost my mother, I lost my best friend. As an only child as well as a fatherless daughter (my father, a dentist, died when I was one and a half years old from a heart attack), I grew up always knowing I was a little different from my peers. My mother chose never to remarry because she did not want anyone else raising her child. All of her energies went into providing for me as best she could.

My mother instilled a sense of independence in me from day one. Given her situation, a widow and mother in the early fifties, I doubt anyone would have questioned her parenting had she swung toward overprotective behavior. She did not, and for that I will be eternally grateful.

What has kept me on course these past twenty-plus years since my mother's death has been (1) a very loving and supportive family who has never held back tears when discussing the impact of her loss; (2) a core group of friends who either knew my mother or who were sensitive enough to ask me about her; and (3) a deep inner drive from within to enjoy life and succeed—a fitting way to honor her memory!

Until recently, I felt that I had worked through just about all there was to work through as it related to mourning for my mother. I was wrong. Something happened to me during a self-defense course. We were asked to develop a "custom conversation scenario" whereby we would have the class "mugger" represent our worst nightmare, be it realistic or symbolic. The idea is that unless we free up the opponent within, we will otherwise ensure failure.

I had the mugger represent cancer. For the first time since my mother's death I yelled and screamed at the disease. I was able to verbalize at a very loud pitch, in the company of a very supportive staff and fellow course members, just how destructive the disease had been. The scenario ended up with me knocking out the disease (the mugger) before it consumed me. I had no idea just how much emotion had been churning within me. What a catharsis!

I still fear the onset of cancer, but I'm starting to view age fifty-four differently—not as an ending, but perhaps as a new beginning.

LINDA,
*thirty-nine, whose mother died of colon cancer twenty-one years ago*

My mom died just three months shy of my eighteenth birthday. She had colon cancer and lived long enough to see her two oldest children graduate from high school, something she never did and always regretted.

I'm the only daughter (with five brothers), and like so many women you interviewed, I had to take care of my brothers from an early age. My youngest brother was barely a year old when our mother was diagnosed and turned four just three weeks after her death. There were so many feelings that I felt I had to hide. I didn't want to get my brothers upset; they needed me. My dad had all he could handle coping with his own feelings, never mind being able to deal with a girl, soon to be a woman.

One of the saddest memories I have of the time was the day she went into the hospital for the last time. It was the only time she had to go by ambulance, and one of the kids in the neighborhood told my six-year-old brother, "Your mother is gonna die!" Of course he came running to me in tears. All I could do was hold him and tell him, "I don't know." Even now that hurts.

I held all my feelings in for about seven years, until one morning I woke up with chest pains. Nothing was physically wrong with me, so I was sent to a therapist who helped me to deal with my anger about my mother's death.

I am six weeks shy of forty now, the age my mother was when she was diagnosed. Needless to say, I have become slightly phobic about it, experiencing symptoms similar to my earlier episodes.

Again, there is no physical cause for this, and I am about to reenter therapy in an effort to deal with it.

*Motherless Daughters* couldn't have been published at a better time, at least for me and my husband, who is reading it now in an effort to better understand what I am going through.

## GINA,
*thirty-five, whose mother died of breast cancer twenty-two years ago*

My mother died after a two-year bout with breast cancer at the age of forty-two. As I read your story, I was angry that practically ten years later the disease still had the same characteristics, taking women like your mother in two years at the same age as mine.

I had just turned thirteen two weeks before my mother passed away. Although much of that time is now a blur of emotions and isolated events, I do remember feeling so out of it. Connected and not connected. Confused. I was the oldest; my two sisters and brother were eleven, seven, and eight years old, respectively.

My dad, whom I consider a truly incredible man, vowed to raise four young children on his own. And he did. When I think back, though, growing up was incredibly difficult. I remember thinking,

"This wouldn't be such a problem if Mommy were around." Whether it was makeup, clothes, or boys, I felt like I was sailing in completely new seas where the captain of the ship was as clueless as I was. My dad did the very best he could, which by most standards today, even for children who have two parents, was damn good. Still, there were gaps and holes and confusion. Your book helped me be able to start looking at those areas and not feel as if I am betraying my father. I can't be angry at a man whose love and devotion were always so obvious, but I can be angry that there were areas he could not fill in, through no fault of his own.

Today I am thirty-five years old and very single. Although I long to be married and to have children, I just haven't seemed to have the luck. Recently, I started looking around at all my friends who are married and having families, and comparing their lives to mine. Why do they seem to be entitled, while that part of happiness still eludes me? I know it was no mere accident that my mother's three daughters are still single (ages thirty to thirty-five), while her son is very happily married. And I know it probably has to do with my early loss. My sense of independence; my desire to achieve all that my mother hadn't in her lifetime; my fear of loss and of being left; my incredibly tough standards for men . . . all have contributed to my situation as a single woman. How to change that still confounds me. But

I feel that maybe now I know where the problem lies.

After many years of searching for a place for myself, I am now a middle-school teacher. I live three thousand miles away from my roots and my dad, sisters, and brother. In the four years I have been teaching, I have had contact with children whose mothers died during their middle-school years. This year, a student with whom I had developed a very close rapport lost her mother to lung cancer. Unlike my reactions to other students' losses, my reaction to Jennifer's loss was incredibly intense. I wanted so much to be there and to help and guide, and yet I was even more upset because of all the things I know lie ahead for this very dynamic young girl. I can't help with those things. I also know what strength and independence and determination she will develop; I see it happening already.

She came back to school two days after her mom died, in an effort (I think) to capture some normalcy and get some attention for her grief. That morning, she and I spent a few hours walking around campus talking and sharing experiences. Not only do I think and hope it helped her, but I know it helped me to give something back to the world. When my mother passed away, it was one of my seventh grade teachers who, with just a smile and a hug, provided some much-needed comfort. All of this makes me wonder if there are truly any "accidents" in my life . . .

When I moved away from my family almost eight years ago, I was finally able to deal with a lot of the grief. Before that, I felt that if I dealt with my grief openly, I would somehow add to my family's. I just couldn't make things more difficult for my dad (who remained single all these years) or for my siblings. Three thousand miles away, I gave myself permission to grieve. The mourning comes in waves, depending on what major event or age I am passing through. I have been in and out of therapy and know this will probably be a lifelong process.

## ROSEMARY,
*thirty-six, whose mother died of asthma and heart failure twenty-three years ago*

I don't think I fully understood the impact of my loss for fourteen years. When I was twenty-seven, I was diagnosed with breast cancer. While I was in the hospital after a lumpectomy, I had a bad reaction to the anesthesia, and my release date was delayed. I was in my room alone when a woman appeared. She said she had heard I wasn't feeling well and wanted to come see me. She looked at me and said, "You look like a motherless child." I was stunned, because at the moment I realized I was one. It didn't matter that my dad had been great (and had even waltzed me around the hospital corridor the night before the surgery), or that my family and friends had been very supportive. I realized that I needed that maternal warmth surrounding me. She held me and we talked about faith—her from a black Baptist perspective, and me from a Jewish/Taoist/New Age-ish one. We spoke for maybe fifteen minutes and then she left. By the next day, I was well enough to go home. I sought her out and found her in bed. It seems she had had a mastectomy the day before she came to help me out, and was feeling the effects of it that day. I was very proud to sit with her among her family and hold her hand and tell her how much she meant to me. Even now, almost ten years later, I am grateful for her presence in my life.

I think, perhaps, it is the experience of finding myself alone, without a guide through the labyrinth of a woman's life, that is the essence of being a motherless daughter to me. I have many women friends ranging from contemporaries to women in their fifties, and friends of the family in their seventies, but knowing what it would have been like for my own mother might have helped me face life differently. I am now contacting friends of my parents and getting their perspective on my mom. It's interesting to find that twenty-three years later I have become someone much like her. I love hearing about her generosity and fearlessness, but equally important is hearing about her insecurities, which somehow make my own more understandable. I appreciate finding her in me, and finding the parts of me which are unique to me.

I find I miss my mother the most when life changes occur, such as when I see my body aging, and as I watch all my friends getting married, and when I turned thirty. I also miss her when life feels a bit overwhelming and I wish I didn't *need* to be so self-sufficient. Much of the time I don't consciously "miss" her, but there are times when I would just love to sit down to tea and cookies and just talk—about anything and everything.

## BARBARA,

*thirty-six, whose mother died after a stroke twenty-three years ago*

My mother died suddenly when I was only thirteen and she was only forty-seven. I am the youngest of three children. My sister was twenty-three then and my brother twenty-six. Both of them were still single at the time. My brother and sister both have had the same reaction you mention at being the age our mother was when she died. My brother said he never felt so relieved as he did when he turned forty-eight. In our family, we had several relatives die in their forties, and we feel that if we can make it to fifty, we are home free. My son is now the age I was when my mother died, and we have discussed this. My father is still alive and well at seventy. He remained a widower for twelve years, not remarrying until I was twenty-five, a mother myself, and already divorced. I am grateful that he did not bring another woman into the house when I was a teenager. He did not feel ready until the time he remarried, and the marriage was for companionship in his old age. From the way he talks and acts, I can see that my mother remains the love of his life.

I think the best way to proceed with this letter is to comment point by point on what really touched me about your book.

1. "I can no longer hear her voice . . ." This is one thing that really gets to me—that try as I may, I can't remember the sound of my mother's voice. This was lost to me within two or three years after she died. I regret that no one thought to get her voice on tape. But I believe that if she could somehow call me on the phone from the beyond, I would immediately recognize her voice after twenty-three years.

2. "At each milestone a daughter comes up against new challenges she's frightened to face without a mother's support, but when she reaches out for her, the mother isn't there." The last milestone I

had with my mother was my first period, which happened only two weeks before her death. I remember going to school the next day, having severe cramps, and having the school nurse call her at home to come get me. I remember watching for the light-green '65 Buick Electra to pull up. I mourned when my father sold that car a year after her death. It was another link to her gone. I missed her terribly when I was married and when my son was born. This was even more so because I lived far away from all my relatives except my father. I had no female relatives nearby to offer support. As the youngest child and as the one who never did any babysitting, I can remember being afraid to be left alone with the baby. This feeling lasted for several months. Fortunately, my ex-husband was the seventh of eleven children and knew just how to take care of a baby.

But some of the worst feelings surrounding milestones come with the ones never reached. I sometimes am glad my mother did not have to see me alone at thirty-six. I was married for only a year and a half after I graduated from high school. My sister is forty-six and pretty much in the same boat. Neither one of us has ever had a decent job we enjoyed, and we are glad she didn't have to see that, either. Our lives are quite different from the happy life that she led. Though she died young, she died secure in the knowledge that my father truly loved her. I am still waiting for the first man to say those three magic words.

3. "Others cling to keep the loss—and their mothers—alive." My brother and sister were quite angry with my father when he sold some of the furniture that my mother had picked out. He did so because six years after her death, his job had transferred him again, and he was buying a smaller house. He did give them some pieces, but they thought he ought to keep every little thing, not realizing how hard it was for him to see these vivid reminders of her each day. He saved one piece for me, an antique bookcase, that I am looking at as I write. More recently, we saw the passings of Richard Nixon and Jackie Kennedy as more of my mother's world slipping away. This hit my sister especially hard. She cried more for my mother than for Jackie when Mrs. Kennedy died. This was because my mother especially loved Mrs. Kennedy and imitated her style of large sunglasses. (I have that last pair of sunglasses my mother wore, and when I put them on, it's like looking at her in the mirror.)

4. "The daughter . . . may . . . become determined to win the war against body image that her mother lost." My mother went on a crash diet the summer before she died. She ate nothing but hamburger meat cooked a certain way. I believe that this diet contributed to her death by weaken-

ing her heart and that she probably would not have had the stroke if she hadn't dieted. I am militantly anti-diet and am active in the size acceptance movement. My mother was 5'8" and weighed around 180 pounds. She wore a size 16/18 before her diet. She paid for the weight loss of 40 pounds and the ability to wear a size 12 with her life. She was also a smoker, and today none of her children smoke.

5. The Youngest Child. I was the "baby," and to this day when I am in the company of my sister, I suddenly feel like a kid again. My mother had her stroke at my aunt's house, and they wouldn't let me come to the hospital with them after the paramedics left. I was left at the house alone for nearly twenty-four hours. This was the most agonizing twenty-four hours of my life. I knew my mother was going to die when I saw them carry her out. I spent the time praying that I was wrong, that I didn't know what I was talking about. Finally, one of my older cousins came and took me to another aunt's house, but I was never allowed to visit my mother in the hospital for the three days it took her to die. *I never got to say good-bye*. I was nearly fourteen; I knew what was going on and I resented being treated as if I were four. When my grandmother on my father's side died sixteen years later, I took my son to the hospital to say good-bye, even though he was six

at the time. I have never shielded him from death. I have presented it as a part of life. Today, I am especially sensitive about being left out in many types of situations.

6. "Now when I'm reminded that I lack the bits of social and personal knowledge other women seem to have absorbed in their mothers' homes, I feel somehow incomplete. Deficient. Wrong." This is *not* me at all. I feel that this is the only benefit of being without a mother during my teens. I feel lucky that I had less indoctrination into stereotyped "femininity" than other women. I feel this lack allowed me to question commonly held assumptions and fostered the growth of my individual humanity. I feel proud that I am not a generic woman, but an individual female human being. I wear my lack of knowledge of "femininity" like a badge. I brag of my inability to cook and sew and of being unable to walk in high heels and of my disdain for makeup. But my mother was not really the froufrou type of woman, either, though she, too, was a home-maker. She was a very fun woman, and her legacies to me were a love of music and art and the encouragement that I could be anything I wanted to be. As a little girl, I loved *The Andy Griffith Show*, and she bought me a little sheriff's badge, which I played with along with my Barbie dolls. A woman at work once told me that I "didn't

know how to be a woman" because I lost my mother so young. She said this because I didn't wear makeup or have an elaborate hairstyle and had no interest in doing either. Well, I have always believed I was born female and that no matter what I did, I would grow up to be a woman, that there wasn't any "how" about it. I told this woman that in the thirteen years my mother and I had together she taught me more important things than how to conform to sex roles. She taught me love, compassion, integrity, humor, and other lasting, real qualities. And my father finished the job by helping me grow up to be a decent human being.

7. ". . . mothers tend to share their stories slowly, meting them out as they deem appropriate for a daughter's current developmental stage." I feel there is so much I don't know about my mother as a human being. I have asked her sister all kinds of things about her, but it isn't the same as hearing it straight from my mother. I wish that she had kept some kind of journal—I would have seen her from her own eyes that way. I have kept a journal for nineteen years, since I was seventeen. I want to be more than just a name and a picture to my descendants.

8. I am very much like Gloria, mentioned on page 254. I have never babied my son, and I view parenthood as a widening sense of independence

for the child. I am not going to be one of those mothers who clings obsessively to her grown children, no matter how lonely I might be. I hope to be close to my son, but I will allow him to live his own life.

## MAY,
*thirty-nine, whose mother died of cancer twenty-three years ago*

My mother died when I was sixteen years old. I was also adopted, so my biological mother "left," too. She agreed while pregnant with me that she would give me to my parents.

To me, being motherless always meant being older than I felt. I felt small and young, more vulnerable because my mother had died. For a while, I forced myself into activities that mimicked a mother's role. I hated it. I enjoyed subsequent teenage delinquency more. I was pleased to do errands for a compassionate teacher and to hate the rest of school. I was already imbued with my mother's values, so even though I ran, or led, the wild pack of boys into the city for a late-night rush, I knew I'd return to bed, to sleep, as a virgin. Things felt heavy, profound, confusing, and all of it pissed me off. Thank God for the openness and love of the 1960s and 1970s. There were many creative, intelligent, political, and spiritual alternatives to following the destructive stereotypes I had been raised with.

I find I am most satisfied with nurturing, caring partners. Perhaps before my mother's death I sought partners who resembled my father, the same male stereotype, but the male and female partners I have had since then and the friends I keep are all nurturing. That was more my mother's quality than my father's, and healthier, too. However, I have the opportunity now to have a great lesbian relationship and I'm hesitating, afraid because this woman's love for me (and for life) is so deep. I don't think I've had this kind of deep love since my mother, and I'm cautious about embracing it now.

I believe my mourning period for my mother will never be complete. I will never *not* mourn this loss, but I am not "in mourning." At thirty-nine, I have more courage to feel pain and share it. I've grown up. I wish she were here to appreciate it with me.

JANET,
*thirty-six, whose mother died in a private plane crash*
*twenty-four years ago*

My mother died when I was twelve years old. Since she died an accidental death and my father (who died eleven months before her) died from heart disease, my father is the one whose death gives me the most personal worry. But my mother's death served to crystallize my awareness of death. She was very good to have around when my father died, and she managed to squelch any fears or worries I harbored because of his death. Unfortunately, that meant when she died I was totally defenseless and unprepared, as if I had never lost a parent.

That is when the nightmares started, and I began thinking about death pretty much all the time. I am hyper-aware that death can come at any time, to anyone, which makes me careful to notice life and enjoy it. Unfortunately, it also makes me unnecessarily morbid, and I'm constantly preparing for the unexpected, which is a waste of time. My mother's death made me superstitious about the sorts of things that make people "knock wood"; I tend to try very hard not to offend "them" (whoever causes things to happen). This gives my husband no end of amusement, in a kind way, and his reaction helps keep me from going overboard.

Not having a mother since I was twelve has meant that I missed a lot of the basics. Sometimes that's not so bad. I'm a terrible ironer, so my husband does it all, and I'm a lousy housekeeper, which is fine because life's too short to bother rearranging dust. Sometimes, though, I'm keenly aware of things my mother would have taught me that I didn't work out on my own until my thirties: simple social customs that everyone knows but me—reciprocal invitations, hostess manners, etc., that can be interpreted as rudeness instead of ignorance.

My mother was a very strong woman, very opinionated, outgoing, and demonstrative. She was involved in everything, mostly for our benefit. (When I told her I didn't want to be a career Girl Scout like my older sister, she heaved a sigh and said she could finally quit the Girl Scout Council.) I was young enough when she died that I still thought she was the voice of right on everything, and I never questioned her opinions. To this day I'll notice that some silly belief I've had all my life is one of her ideas, and it's totally fallacious. Some were obvious and discarded when I was still in my teens (such as "redheads can't wear pink"), and some I just jettisoned last week ("babies shouldn't be picked up every time they cry"). If she were still alive, we'd probably be going around and around about most everything, because heredity or environment has given me her spirit. I'm just as opinionated and outgoing, although, I believe, more tolerant. I am a confident woman, which I believe is her gift to me. She supported me and bolstered me and helped me build a tremendous amount of self-esteem in the twelve years I spent with her. Very few people can get me down or bend me to their will, but I know for a fact that if she were alive, she would be able to push my buttons with deadly accuracy. I don't know if she would, but I know she definitely could.

My mother-in-law has always considered me less—less socially acceptable, less mannered, less like regular people. I think I was the first orphan she knew, and I had to be, by definition, a charity case. She couldn't relate to someone who spoke her own mind, lived her own life, knew where she was going, and what she wanted. Instead of recognizing that as a personality type, she blamed my motherless condition. In her opinion, my mother would have taught me how to hold my peace, to knuckle under for appearance sake, to speak and move like a "lady," and to never tell anyone how I really felt. That's the way people work in her family. Lucky for her, she never met my mother. I've often watched as my mother squared off with her in my fantasies. My engagement, college summers, my wedding: my mother would have minced her in moments, not in the pointed, articulate way I would have hoped for, but in her own bulldozer way, the same way she mowed down all the people who treated any of her children unfairly or cruelly.

My mother has been dead nearly twenty-five years. Her death has made me independent, caused me to take responsibility for myself, and allowed me to make my own choices. But I still miss her almost every day. I still feel some anger toward her for dying, and guilt for the anger I showed her the day she died. She's never met my terrific husband or my beautiful son. She's never here when I need to be folded up in her arms. When I cry for my parents, it's my mother I want. When I need a person like me, someone who's honest and direct, she isn't here. She's not on the end of a phone line. She's nowhere.

## JOANNE,

*thirty-three, whose mother died of alcoholism twenty-four years ago*

My mother died when I was nine years old, and at nearly thirty-four years of age, I agree it changes everything. My family cannot seem to speak about my mother in any realistic way. My father only describes her as a warm and "glowing" woman who loved her babies. Her father can speak of her childhood now without too much pain, but her adult life is a mystery to me.

My mother lost a baby boy to spina bifida when I was four years old, and was told by a doctor at that time that his death was her fault. I feel that this is when my mother truly died. She was able to be a mother to her children before this incident, but afterwards she was only attempting to stop the pain of living. As a result, I know very little of my mother. My older brother remembers her loving certain nursery rhymes and singing him to sleep. I only remember her drinking.

I have found many photos of her that are so strikingly like myself—in physical ways, like gestures and postures—that they seem eerie. At times I feel as if I'm a photocopy or a ghost of who she must have been at one time. A counselor once told me that she must have been quite a special person to have affected so many people so deeply. But no one is able to speak of who she was or what she was like.

The special bond between mother and child existed between us even through the alcoholism. Her kindness remained, and she seemed to be a person dying of some strange cancer rather than from drink.

When she died, it was as if all that I had trusted was ripped out of my life. Now, as a mother myself, I find that at times I hold back. I love my daughter fiercely, but I find a sense of sadness in that, as if it makes me more vulnerable to future pain. My attempts at relationships are always a search for the mother that died. I am constantly reminded that I have no one I can go to when I need to be held. I wonder at times if the feelings I have when holding my daughter are different from other women who hold their daughters, women who don't need extra love from their daughters because they have a source in a living mother. I try to assess every relationship and gesture on my part to see if I am expecting too much, or hoping for too much in the way of a deep connection between hearts.

What you say is true: losing a mother was not "meant" to happen. It strengthens us and gives us character, but I for one am tired of being strong. I'd give it all up for being wrapped in her scent and her hug.

MARLENE,
*forty-three, whose mother died of breast cancer twenty-five years ago*

My mother had breast cancer for five years and died at the age of fifty-one, two weeks before my nineteenth birthday. My father died suddenly six years later at the age of sixty-one, just nine days after my twenty-fifth birthday. I have felt alone ever since.

In 1964, diagnosis and treatment were not as sophisticated as today's medicine. My mother did not have a palpable lump. Only after she had back pain for six months did her doctor admit her to the hospital for evaluation. When her cancer was finally diagnosed, she was given six months to live. My father and mother's two sisters chose not to tell my mother of her prognosis. They knew she would be devastated, since she was terrified of "The Big C." She was not one to complain and did whatever the doctors thought best. By some miracle, she lived longer than expected. My father was not honest with my two brothers or me. My older brother, who is eight years older than my twin brother and I, has always seemed more like another father than a brother. During my mother's illness, he alternated between living on his own and living with the family. My twin brother, who is one minute older, treated me more like a substitute mother than an equal sister.

Not until the end of the summer of 1967, when my mother took a turn for the worse, did we find out the severity of her illness. Luckily, a new doctor was found who admitted my mother to the hospital. He was able to prolong her life for two more years. Somehow, we still had to keep the secret from her. Each day, I wondered if this was going to be the day my mother died. I was terrified each time when I came home from school that I would find her dead. Years later, when I asked one of my aunts why we didn't get counseling, she told me my father had refused, for fear my mother would discover the truth.

While my mother was sick, and because I was the only girl, it was my responsibility to take care of Mommy. Whenever my mother was unable to do housework and cook the meals, it was my job to do them. In that era, boys were not expected to help in the house. During my teenage years, I was consumed with my mother's illness instead of the usual things other girls my age were experiencing. Our lives were built around whether Mommy was having a good or a bad day. We had to put up with strangers in our apartment who were hired to assist Mommy after her multiple surgeries. If we complained, we were told to shut up. The only thing that mattered was my mother. I felt that my twin brother's and my feelings didn't count. Our teachers were not informed of the situation at home, so they kept complaining that we weren't working up to our potential. My father would just criticize and tell us to work harder, not realizing that our home life was affecting our grades.

I chose to become a nurse to help others. During my sophomore year at nursing school, my mother died. Our religious mourning period ended on Thanksgiving Day. I had to return to school the following Monday. There was no time to grieve. People expected me to be over the death after the designated seven-day period. Little did I realize that I would be mourning for the rest of my life. Somehow I had to gather the energy to keep going. To this day, I do not know how I managed to return to my clinic rotation on the breast cancer ward of the hospital. I know I was angry at the women who neglected their lumps and were now dying, but in order to give them good nursing care, I had to bury those feelings.

My father was the distant father who did not know how to mourn. I think he had never recovered from his own parents' deaths. His father had died very quickly in 1942 of pancreatic cancer. Supposedly, it was a horrible death. Watching his wife linger for such a long time took a tremendous toll on him. He was a workaholic who turned to me and said, "Because you are the girl in the family, you are responsible to perform all the household duties." I felt I had no other choice. I lived at the dormitory during the week and did the household chores on the weekends. My weekends consisted of cleaning the apartment, doing the laundry, going shopping for food, and picking up the dry cleaning. In addition, I had to cook for the week for my father and brother. Somehow I had to fit in homework. During my senior year of college, I worked on Sundays and holidays at a hospital to get additional experience. Whenever I complained that I needed help, my father ignored me. He treated me like his wife. Luckily, he never approached me sexually, but he expected me to do everything else my mother had done for him. He would let the phone ring once when he left work so that I would have dinner waiting for him when he came home.

My father was very cold. He never complimented us on anything we did; he only found fault. He never hugged us or said he loved us. On occasion, he wanted me to accompany him to the movies or a concert. When someone suggested that he start dating, he said he wouldn't find another woman like his wife and, besides, he wasn't ready. He turned my mother into a saint. After I graduated in 1972, my father told me that the only way I could have a normal life was to move out of his house. If I stayed, I would be expected to continue to do the housework. When I found a job and an apartment, my father would not help me move.

After my mother died, my father assumed my mother's sisters would be like another mother to us, but they had their own families, and I always was the one who had to ask for help. Only after they finished doing for their own children would they try to find the time for me. I became tired of being placed second. It is as if I had to wait around for the bread crumbs of attention when children with mothers got the whole loaf of bread. This caused me to become independent and not rely on others.

I met my husband in 1973. He was the first person to put me first. When my roommates left a mess, he told me I did not have to clean for them.

He would take me out to dinner. From the beginning, he could tell that I was not like the other self-centered girls he had known. I only knew how to cater to men. He seemed to appreciate my domestic skills and raved about my cooking. So when we were married in 1974, I continued the pattern I had established at home. My husband expected me to treat him like a king, the same way his mother treated his father. She told him that when he married, his wife would do everything for him. Years later, I became tired of caring for everyone else. I wanted someone to take care of me.

My mother-in-law liked me right away. She kept telling me I was just like another daughter to her. I was happy to find another mother. During this time my husband's younger sister was away at college. We never really had a chance to get to know each other. When I visited my in-laws' home, my mother-in-law and I would go shopping. I just ate up all the attention and mothering. I only wanted to please his parents and maintain their love, so I did everything to make them happy, losing my identity in the process.

My husband went into the air force soon after graduation in 1975. A week before we were to move, my father died unexpectedly. Since the family decided they did not want an autopsy, I can only assume it was a heart attack. My twin brother found him dead when he went to investigate why he was not getting ready for work. It was quite a shock—

not just his death, but also becoming an orphan at the age of twenty-five.

Once again, I did not have time to mourn. I wanted to stay behind and help my twin brother in the apartment, but my husband told me my place was with him. After our move, I noticed a change in my mother-in-law's attitude. Being 1,200 miles away, I am sure, made it difficult. We spoke every week, but I did not tell her how much I was hurting. Many nights I cried myself to sleep. There were many problems between my brothers concerning my father's estate, but I kept the phone conversations to my in-laws happy and light.

I became pregnant two months after moving, and I expected everyone to be excited over my pregnancy and to make me feel special. When my sister-in-law became engaged two weeks after I made my announcement, my in-laws' focus shifted to the wedding. My doctor would not permit me to fly back home for the wedding because of an early bleeding problem in the pregnancy. At the time, I felt very lonely. My husband would not become involved with my pregnancy either. I cried the entire weekend he went up north for his sister's wedding. Since he was the only person around, I expected him to make a fuss over me as husbands do on television or in the movies. I realize now what a burden I put on him. It was not possible for him to give me all the love I needed. He was also too immature to accept the responsibility of fatherhood. My mother-in-law gave excuses why she could not come and help me when the baby came. There was no such thing as baby nurses where I lived. I was alone postpartum to care for my daughter.

After my husband finished his two years in the air force, we moved back north. I wanted my daughter to know her only grandparents. We lived in their home for six months until my husband decided where he would set up his practice. This situation was not difficult for him because we were living in what had been his home. For me, it was uncomfortable because I was the visitor and guardian of a toddler. I was always afraid of doing the wrong thing. What made it more difficult was that I had no family or friends in the area. We only had one car, which my husband took to work. I felt like a prisoner. My mother-in-law would go shopping and not ask me to join her. When she came home, she would ask what was for dinner. Once again I felt taken advantage of. When my sister-in-law gave birth two years later, my mother-in-law went to her home out of state for two weeks to help her and told me to take care of her husband. She said she was forced to go, because otherwise the other grandmother would go and she would look bad. That did not make me feel any better. I began to see a difference in the way she treated her daughter and the way she treated me. Whenever my sister-in-law visited, she and her mother would do things and not include me. I was hurt. After all, I had been told I was like another daughter.

My twenty-ninth year was my worst. I had two miscarriages six months apart. At that time, miscarriages were not considered a loss. After the second miscarriage I became very depressed. I felt burdened with so many losses in my young life. This is when I finally started to mourn my parents. My husband was relieved to be released from the financial responsibility of another child at that time. He was struggling to establish himself in his practice. I wanted to talk, but no one wanted to listen. Everyone just said to get on with my life.

I knew mentally I couldn't stand another miscarriage or loss, so I made sure I was healthy and there were no pathological reasons for the miscarriages before I became pregnant again. When I learned I was pregnant with my son, it was the best thirtieth birthday present I could have received. My husband's sister sent me a birthday card with a note saying she was also pregnant and due the day before me. I cried when I read the note. My mother-in-law could not understand why I was not as excited as her daughter. I tried to explain that I was too scared of another miscarriage to allow myself to become excited.

Being pregnant along with my sister-in-law was as awful as I had expected. Once again, my in-laws put all the attention on their daughter. My mother-in-law compared us constantly. I was not supposed to feel tired or nauseous because her daughter did not feel that way. How much weight did I gain? Did the doctor hear the baby's heartbeat? When I realized the games she was playing, I decided not to share any information with her. I could not tell her when I had a doctor's appointment or when I felt the baby kick, for fear that if her daughter had not felt life yet, she would become alarmed. Another situation made me long for my mother: My mother-in-law was torn regarding where to go when the babies were due. I had no one to watch my daughter, whereas my sister-in-law had a mother-in-law who was willing to help her. Naturally, my mother-in-law wanted to be with her daughter. I just kept feeling that if my mother were alive, there would not be any problem.

When my sister-in-law gave birth nine days before me, my mother-in-law felt trapped because she could not go to her daughter until I gave birth. I called my mother-in-law to congratulate her on her new granddaughter, and I could tell she was crying. When I asked her why, she told me it was because her daughter had a daughter. I cried, too, because there was no one to cry for me. After I came home from the hospital, my mother-in-law stayed for a while. She kept telling me three times a day how she should have gone to her daughter's. After all, her daughter didn't want her mother-in-law, she wanted her mother. My son had colic and I wasn't getting any rest, but I was doing more than I should have because my husband didn't want his mother working too hard.

My husband's grandmother made me feel even worse. She came to me and cried because her husband, the great-grandfather, did not live to see this great-grandson. I responded how upset I was that my parents didn't make it, either. My husband's family has never been sensitive to my feelings. It took me years to realize that no one can replace my parents. I expected too much from my in-laws.

My twin brother's wife told me something her father has told her: Parents are like the covers on a book. When the covers fall off, the pages start to tear away. Once the parents are gone, holding the family together becomes very difficult. Since my brothers' wives have their parents, they celebrate holidays with them. What I miss most about my youth is the feeling of belonging to a large family on a holiday. It is at these times that being an orphan is most painful.

I miss my mother so much more than my father. She was the one who gave me love. I envy the girls in the mall out shopping with their mothers and children. It has been difficult for my husband to understand the sense of loss I feel, or to understand why I cannot stop mourning. I requested that he

read your book so that he could have a better understanding. When he finished it, he admitted that you
and I share many of the same feelings. He now
seems to have better insight into the way I think and
feel.

## ADORA,

*thirty, whose mother died of leukemia twenty-five years
ago*

I lost my mom when I was five years old, ready to
turn six. She died three days before my birthday, at
the age of twenty-seven. My dad was seventeen years
older than she. He loved and adored her very much.

After her death, I felt that I was living in hell. I
went from losing my mother into being sexually
abused by my older brother. The abuse actually
started before she died. My brother, Roger, first in-
cested me when I was four years old. I have three
older half-brothers and one half-sister. Immediately
after my mom died, the abuse picked up. My father
would leave me and my two-year-old brother in the
care of my older brothers and sister. Dad was always
busy working, and was never around to stop what
was happening to me. My other brothers knew that
Roger was touching me and making me do things I

didn't want to do, but they did nothing about it except join in on the abuse.

In a way, I blamed my mother for leaving me. If she hadn't died, I know I eventually would have told her about the abuse. As it turned out, the abuse didn't stop until I was twelve years old. My dad had remarried when I was seven to my stepmother, Connie, who had a daughter named Pam. Pam was the same age I was when she and her mom came into my life. My brothers started abusing her, too, but she was scared to say anything about it. Neither of us told Connie until I started having nightmares. That's when I told Connie about what Roger was doing to me and Pam. She was furious about it. I remember sitting down at the kitchen table with Connie and Roger. Roger admitted to what he did, and Connie told him to get out of the house. That night I had no choice but to tell my dad about the abuse, because he didn't understand why Roger had been kicked out. When I told him, he said he knew that his boys were touching me, but he didn't know they were touching Pam. Connie was again furious that he did nothing to stop his daughter from being abused, let alone her daughter. My dad said it was normal for boys and girls to touch each other. They did a lot more than just touch me, but he didn't want to hear that.

Instead of getting better, my nightmares got worse. I started dreaming about my mom telling me

I was a bad girl for letting my brothers touch me. She said that's why she left me. At the same time I was having these dreams, I remembered how my dad finally told me about my mom's death. He had kept it from me for seven months, telling me that she went away on a trip. One day I was asking him questions about death. We were at my grandmother's house, playing in the pool, and I asked what would happen to me if I held my breath underwater for too long. My dad thought this was a good time to tell me that my mom wasn't coming home.

I didn't remember this until I was twelve and having those nightmares about my mom. I guess I'd blocked out that whole day. I think from that time on, even with the abuse happening, I separated from myself and from my body. That's when I started blocking out bits and pieces of my life that I didn't want to remember, especially the parts about abuse.

I've had to work through a lot of shit because of that family. After my stepmom died seven years ago, I felt like my whole life was ending again. My dad had called me at midnight, the day after Thanksgiving, to tell me Connie had died. She was a diabetic for the last seven years and it finally took her life. I loved her, but not as much as I loved my own mother. Connie abused me also, physically and mentally. That night when she died, I went outside to wait for my dad and Pam. Once the cold air hit me, I went hysterical in the middle of the street, crying for my mother. Not for Connie, who'd just died, but for my mother. It was like I was grieving for her all over again.

I did drugs and used alcohol after Connie died. I was in bad relationships, feeling totally numb when I slept with men and letting them abuse me, too. Why not? I was numb. I felt nothing until I landed in a mental institute five years ago. I was in a rehab program for a month, and then I felt everything. Talk about feeling overwhelmed. I relived everything— my mother's death, the sexual abuse, my addictive relationships, and my drug and alcohol use.

Now, I'm a happily married woman. I'm still working through my mother's death and its effect on me, but I'm not repeating the self-destructive patterns anymore. I've learned a lot about myself and the people who were in my life and the people who aren't in my life anymore.

As you may be able to tell, I'm still very bitter and angry about the shit that has happened to me. And you know who I blame? My dear old dad, who has never been a father to me, who was never even there to protect or care for me. Just a few years ago, I took away the most precious thing that he holds dear to him—me. I did not give him the privilege of giving me away at my wedding. He had to sit with the rest of the family and watch my father-in-law give me away to his son. My in-laws have shown me more love than my own family ever did. I have nothing more to do with the Brecht family. I'm a Palmer now, and very happy to be a Palmer.

In your book, you talk about abandonment issues. I deal with that every day. I'm always scared that when my husband goes to work or goes out to be with his friends that he's not going to come home to me. Either he's going to find another woman or he's going to get into a car accident. This November it's going to be three years since we got married. He's sworn to love me forever, and he hasn't been in a car accident yet, but I'm terrified to lose him. He's the first man to love me unconditionally, and he won't even lay a hand on me to hurt me in any way. My husband knows about my past and hates my father with a passion. But I don't know how to get past my fear of abandonment.

The whole point of writing this letter is to tell my secrets, because I don't have to keep my abuse or my losses a secret anymore. I want to help other adults and children, to give them hope that there is a God who loves them, and that it isn't God's will for a child to lose a parent or to be abused by anyone on this earth. If a man chooses to sexually abuse a child, it's not God's fault or the child's fault. The perpetrator is responsible for his own actions, and he's the one who pays in the end. I'm not quite done working through my issues from the past, but I truly believe my father and my brothers are paying for what they did to me. They're no longer allowed to be a part of my life.

## LOIS,
*thirty-six, whose mother died of colon cancer twenty-six years ago*

For the past twenty-six years I have been a mother-less daughter. Also, for the past ten years I have been a parentless daughter.

I'm the youngest of three children. My sister is eighteen years older than I, and my brother is four years older. I was a late baby—Mom was forty-three and Daddy was fifty-one when I came along. My brother and I are close, whereas my sister and I are not. It has always been that way.

Mom had colon cancer that soon spread through her body. The last year that she was alive, after having the disease for five years, she was more in the hospital than out of it. The last time I remember her being home was for my ninth birthday . . . and then only for a couple of days before being rushed back to the hospital and surgery, again.

I'll never forget being awakened at 6:30 that morning in 1969 by my daddy and our minister, who is a very good friend of the family—almost a member of the family. That was when I was told

Mom had died two hours earlier. A girlfriend had slept overnight with me, so she was there when I got the news. It was hard for me to keep from screaming and crying. My daddy and our minister just kept holding me and letting me cry as much as I wanted to. For the next few days, I was never left alone. Someone was always with me.

I was lucky in a sense after my mom died because for sixteen and a half years I still had my daddy with me. If it hadn't been for him, I wouldn't have survived. Sure, Daddy and I argued and fought with each other and for each other, but I always knew that he loved his little girl until the very end. Daddy never remarried or even dated after Mom's death. When Mom first got cancer, Daddy retired to be at home with her. They were extremely close.

For the sixteen and a half years between Mom's and Daddy's deaths, I had some difficult times. A girl needs her mom then. I personally thought I had cancer when I started my menstrual cycle. Three years later when my periods stopped coming and I knew I couldn't be pregnant, I thought for sure I had cancer and would soon be joining my mom. Years later when I had to have a hysterectomy because of tumors, I again thought of dying of cancer.

I've learned one thing from seeing both parents suffer—Daddy, thank God, only for six weeks, whereas Mom did for five years or longer. I've decided that when my time comes, I want it to go fast, no machines or anything. Just let me die peacefully.

There are certain times I miss my mom the most:

1. When I'm sick, either normally or seriously. Three years ago, I was diagnosed as a Type 1 diabetic. I'm on three insulin shots a day, now. Giving that first shot to myself was frightening. I wished my mom (or Daddy) could have been there, reassuring me, as always, that I would be okay.

2. When I had exciting news. Like now, after thirty-six years, I have finally found the man I want to spend the rest of my life with. It would have been nice to share that with her. My question now is, How does one plan a wedding without parents?

3. On special occasions, like the births of my three nieces and two nephews, and their high school graduations. She would have been so proud.

One thing that helped me cope with my mom's death occurred during my sophomore year of high school. My English teacher did a six-week course on death as it was represented in books and plays, and for the last three weeks of the course we dealt with personal experiences of death. Mrs. Schmidt decided to do the course because four classmates had been killed after a football game in a car wreck a few weeks before. For most of my fellow classmates in that course, losing our four friends was the closest experience they'd had to losing anyone. I, on the other hand, had lost my mom. I didn't talk too much in that class until one day Mrs. Schmidt asked that I stay after class. Her concern was that I was usually so bubbly, always volunteering and talking during all her other assignments, but that for this one I had clammed up. She wanted to know why. It took me a few minutes, but finally I explained what had happened to my mom. Mrs. Schmidt told me she understood, and asked if I wanted to talk openly with the class about it. I told her I did. The next day the dreaded homework assignment was on the board. Each of us would have to stand up in class and tell our classmates what "death" meant to us. I wrote about my mother. I still to this day have that report, with Mrs. Schmidt's comments on it: "Lois, I'm really glad that you can talk about this so freely. It must have been terrible, but I think you have come a long way. Keep it up!!"

The truth is, I never fully realized what my parents' deaths meant to me until just three years ago, when I suddenly lost a job I'd given my all for—or at least I'd thought I had. All of a sudden, I was alone. My roommate kicked me out of our apartment when she heard about my job. I had no place to go, no money saved, so what else was there to do? I tried, very unsuccessfully, I might add, to commit suicide. The only place it got me was eight and a half weeks in the hospital psychiatric ward. I went through extensive therapy, was told I was manic-depressive, put on medication, and sent to group therapy. Once in my group, thanks to a very nice counselor, I let go and told my group about my experience of losing both parents. I felt as if a mountain had been lifted off my chest when I finally, through a flood of tears, could say my parents were *dead*. I'd always thought in the back of my mind that someday they would come walking back into my life. But of course, that never happened.

I am a very affectionate person today, probably too much for my own good. If I like you, you've got a friend for life. I can easily greet a close friend with a kiss on the cheek and a quick hug. I'm not afraid to show my emotions. I watch reunions on TV, and before it's all over I'm crying. Movies have the same effect.

I still find telling someone "good-bye" to be very hard. I cry when I have to tell someone that, but I cry even harder when they come back to me. I never fail to tell my fiancé "I love you" every day. Thank goodness I have him to say that to.

GAYLE,
*forty, whose mother died of cancer twenty-seven years ago*

I recently underwent treatment with a psychiatrist, and I found that the "hole" I was carrying around with me, that space that only a mother can fill, had become large enough to begin interfering with my life.

I just turned forty-one the other day, have a good marriage of seventeen years, one child, and a normal, basic life. I work in a good government job and have never been abused or had any real problems in my life. The two most significant events of my life were my mother's death in the winter of my thirteenth year and my son's diagnosis of diabetes when he was ten months old. The two events were major sources of grief, as you can imagine, but I dealt with my son's diabetes much better than I did with the death of my mom. I was an adult at the time of my son's diagnosis, and you're right: children don't know how to grieve. I still think of myself at the breathless, expectant age of thirteen, and I know I was still very much a child. My point in telling you all of this is to let you see that I am in every other way "normal" (whatever that is), with a happy childhood behind me and a pretty good mainstream life now.

After starting therapy, I realized I needed it some time ago. My sister, who was seven when Mother died, didn't remember much about Mom, so as the years passed I found myself being her memory of Mom. We also have a brother who is four years younger than me. When my sister finally married at the age of thirty-four, I found myself cast in a slightly different role than before. Suddenly little sister didn't seem to need me like she used to. I was unaccountably depressed that summer, although I put on quite a happy face.

I had always felt that after twenty-seven years I shouldn't feel so sad near the anniversary of Mom's death, that I shouldn't feel so empty at the thought of her being gone. But I did. Mostly the pain was muted in my everyday life, but as my son has gotten older and I have told him about her, it's returned. She died of cancer, and I remember everything that happened in the six months she was ill as if it were yesterday. When my son asked innocently if she died of AIDS, what should have been a humorous question was like a knife splitting open a ripe fruit full of grief. I knew I needed help.

I have always had a weight problem, and through therapy I realize that I started stuffing myself with food after my mother's death. I stole money from girls' purses for years after that, and hoarded food. I was convinced that whatever was good in my life wouldn't last, that I had to get what I needed on the sly. My father did his best with three kids and asked my maternal grandmother to live with us to help out. She did so and gave of herself selflessly for four years (a fact she reminds us of, when it's convenient). In an effort to keep things as normal as possible, they didn't show us their grief much, and we continued our school and life activities as before. Only recently have I learned that my father paced the house at night, unable to sleep, and often came home from work early, too broken up to remain at the office. I never knew those things, and I now hurt for him. In their kind but misguided attempt to hide their pain, the message I got was that my grief was somehow too volatile and scary to let out. I *needed* to let it out, but I somehow felt it was undignified and had to remain unexpressed. Consequently, it remained and it surprises me every now and then with its sharpness and intensity.

My mom was thirty-six when she died, and the day I turned thirty-seven was one of the oddest days of my life. My mother actually died four days after turning thirty-six, but the reality of living longer than her didn't hit me until I turned thirty-seven. It was a Sunday, and I was puzzled by my lack of enthusiasm that day. I hadn't started examining and making peace with my inner feelings of loss yet, so they were still a mystery and a source of self-recrimination to me. After some years of unfulfilling employment, I had been working in a terrific, challenging job for about two years at that time and was enjoying professional success. My personal and family life was in good shape; I was overweight but happy in every other area. But I found myself not counting my blessings that day, and I couldn't figure out why.

I looked at my then-ten-year-old son and was overwhelmed by the urge to sob—what would happen to him if I, like my mother, died at this age? He was a loving child and so full of promise and excitement about life. The thought of not seeing him grow to manhood was physically painful. It literally sucked my breath away. I looked at my husband and imagined how lost he would be if I died, and another knife pierced my heart. I found myself mourning the imagined loss of our future together, the plans we'd made, the dreams we'd had, and it felt so real it was frightening. It was like being in a slow-motion train wreck—inevitable and unavoidable—and I couldn't get off. Where the heck did this come from? Instead of being happy for having lived thirty-seven years and contentedly planning for the future, I found myself mired in these morbid thoughts of unreal loss. I felt so guilty about my feelings, I didn't share them with anyone else at the time—keep those dirty little negative outlooks to myself, can't embarrass myself by letting them out.

Perhaps the weirdest occurrence (and funniest, as I look back on it now) was that the *Twilight Zone* theme song kept running through my head all day. I couldn't shake it, and I still don't know what fertile minefield it emerged from. I spent the day absolutely baffled by the power of my grief, rather than celebrating my life. I now know that I was grieving for the losses my mother suffered as she died—including her loss of her future. How awful and terrifying that must have been for her. The sad little thirteen-year-old who lost her mother all those years ago was trying to get out and work through her feelings of loss, too. It took me another couple of years to identify those feelings, and I'm just now feeling okay about feeling lousy about the loss of my mom. I now find myself wondering what Mom would have done with her life after we three kids grew up and left.

I can see now that my need to hide my grief led me to hide other aspects of my life as well. Consequently, I am a closet eater and I buy excessively when things are on sale. Sounds trivial, but I can see the connection, and it's not a healthy response to a sale, believe me. If I couldn't ask openly for something I needed, I'd get it in any way I could—thus the stealing. I remember taking small pleasure in the sympathetic reactions of a couple of friends, including my first boyfriend, shortly after Mom's death. Instead of being comforting, it was yet another source of guilt. What kind of person *enjoys* the attention paid to her because of her mother's death? A quite normal, confused adolescent girl, it turns out.

Although I can remember the events of that time in my life with utter clarity, I cannot remember feeling the grief that surprises me at times now. I can remember standing in the grass outside her first-floor hospital room and talking to her through the window (in 1967 children were not allowed in hospital rooms). I remember getting my very first pair of nylons for the funeral, and the secret pleasure I took in wearing them. I remember the ambulance in the driveway to take her away for the last time, as I arrived home from school. I remember her yellow skin, the sharp cheekbones that I never knew this large, soft woman had, and the sound of her vomiting after drug therapy. I remember the smell of flowers in the funeral home, and how her lipstick was chipped after her body was flown more than two thousand miles for burial. I remember how we kids were scolded for giggling too heartily from exhaustion the day after she was buried. I know now that I hid the pain in the unfortunate belief that we had to "get over it and carry on." With the guidance and insight that therapy has provided me, I can look at that ripe girl of thirteen and feel how terribly she must have hurt. I look at my sensitive fourteen-year-old son and can see myself in him. I imagine how it would absolutely devastate him to lose me, and I see myself at thirteen again. Suddenly the pain is as real as the events were.

I married well, to a stable man who is just now

understanding some of the things I've wrestled with in private for twenty-seven years, and openly only for the last two. All the mother stuff has come out in therapy, although I've always suspected it was there. I still make bad food choices, but this year when the sad fog that accompanies the anniversary of Mom's death surrounded me, I relaxed and let it come. For the first time *ever* the tears I shed were cleansing and somehow comforting. After twenty-seven years, it was okay to feel lousy about losing a mother I adored and relied on. After all these years, I finally thought of that pain as something other than bad and inappropriate. This time it was an identifiable thing, and while it wasn't exactly welcome, I let it wash over me and just felt bad about it for a couple of days. It felt good to acknowledge it without guilt. It felt good to just feel bad. Is this healing? It's too soon for me to tell, but I hope so.

Although my life has not been pathetic because my mom died, her death did affect me in ways I'm just now beginning to understand. I was always a can-do, by-the-bootstraps kind of woman. I think I got that strength mostly because I had to get along after Mom was gone. And that's good. But I was also judgmental: Why couldn't others manage their lives like I did through adversity? I'm softening, learning to accept weaknesses in others, as I'm learning to accept the damaged parts of me.

## CAROLYN,

*forty, whose mother died twenty-eight years ago*

I have met very few motherless daughters, and most people of my acquaintance—including my own sister, who was twenty-six when our mother died—have no idea what impact her death has had on me. They tell me that I exaggerate its effects and that I should be over it already. I often tell myself that they are right, because she died when I was twelve and I'm presently forty. Now I know that the feeling I have of constant fear (that the rug will be pulled out from under me) is shared by others who have experienced such a sudden, devastating loss at an early age, and I don't feel so alone.

I found the tone of your book to be somewhat more positive than one I would have written, perhaps because I lost my father and grandfather, my next two primary caretakers, by the time I was seventeen. I feel that I will always have this sense of impending doom hanging over me. My life has felt like one disaster followed too closely by the next with too little time to rest in between. Consequently, I feel I have achieved much less than what I know I could have if my mother, at least, had lived longer. After experiencing her death, the others were nothing by comparison. We were so close that I know I'll never stop missing her, even though I know she was far from perfect.

I'm presently in one job, unsure of how to embark on a career in another. My career is always secondary to finding ways to help myself feel comforted and caring for my pets, who have truly helped me survive the last twenty years. I never seem to make enough money to pay bills adequately or live comfortably enough to feel safe.

Another thing that pleased me about your book is the fact that you mentioned a percentage of motherless women who are lesbians. I tried to live a "new and improved" version of my mother's life which included marrying a man who even looked like my father, until I came out four months after he and I separated. I still find the overwhelming attraction I feel toward women to be very scary, because it's so powerful and seems to be related to my mother. It's hard enough to come out, but to have sexual feelings related to your "sainted" mother who may be watching you from heaven? Unthinkable. I'm sure that would be quite an interesting area of research for a new book.

KIMM,

*thirty-three, whose mother died of complications from lupus twenty-nine years ago*

I'm thirty-three years old and I still want my mommy.

Three weeks after I turned four my mother died. She was also thirty-three years old. Her death has shaped my life in many ways, but because I just turned the age she was when she died, my emotions surrounding her death are much closer to the surface.

Knowing my mother died at thirty-three made my own thirty-third birthday difficult. I felt as if I were entering uncharted territory. I felt guilty, because it didn't seem fair that I should outlive my mother. I felt sad that my mother was not there for my birthday, but most of all I felt terrified. How was I going to know what decisions to make when my own mother hadn't reached this point in her life?

This was strange. Because both my mother and I were so young when she died, it wasn't as if I was able to watch how she made decisions in her life, so why was I so scared to live past her? I think that even though I was too young to watch and absorb, as long as I was an age my mother had reached I felt a sense of security. My mother had gone to college, gotten married, and had a home during her short life. I had also had these same experiences, so there was a sense of familiarity. But what now? Now that I am older than she ever was, what do I do?

Because of this overwhelming fear, in some strange, subconscious way, I think I created complete chaos in my life. I quit a job I had for three years, gave up my apartment because I thought I'd found a different one, and stopped communicating with a group of friends that I had become rather close to. It felt as if I needed to let go of everything— a sort of death of my first thirty-three years of life.

One way I helped myself through this scary time was by working on a documentary of my mother's life. I gathered pictures, slides, her writings, and anything else I could find about her and put it all together in a video and booklet. While I knew that this video would not bring her back, I was hoping that it would comfort me through these tough times. I was right. Each time that I felt scared or sad, I could spend a half hour in her presence. No, I can't hug my mother through the video, but I can watch this beautiful person on screen, and I somehow sense her warmth again.

Yes, I'm thirty-three years old and I still want my mommy. But in a way, by confronting my deepest pain and fear, I've found her. Whether I'm thirty-three or forty-nine or sixty-three, my mother will always be with me. Together, we will conquer these new, uncharted territories.

## ANGELA,

*thirty-nine, whose mother died of an allergic reaction*
*twenty-nine years ago*

I have seen so many similarities between myself and the women in *Motherless Daughters.* So far the two things that really shook me were the fact that 45 percent of us have remained childless. I felt so much better when I saw that. (Aha! I *knew* that was why I never wanted children!) But what brought the most emotion out in me was your recurring dream, the same dream that I have had for twenty-eight years, that my mother is back, she never really died, it's all a mistake, but she's just *there.* She doesn't seem to be happy to be back or to be apologetic; she's totally emotionless. And I'm flipping out because she was so warm and loving in real life, and I know if she were to come back it wouldn't be like that. Like all the other motherless daughters, I *know* that my mother would never be like that. She was *perfect* and if she were still alive my life would have been *perfect,* no problems, not a one!

About myself: I was ten years old and the youngest child of five when my mother died of an allergic reaction to penicillin the family doctor gave her in our home while I was at school. Talk about a sudden death. She wasn't even sick when I left for school. My brother was ill and the doctor was paying a house call. My mother was having a touch of the flu, though, and the rest is history. The minute I found out about her death from my father ("Honey, Mommy's with God now") I think I knew nothing would ever be normal again. I could go on and on about how screwed up my life has been, but I think to sum it up, the worst of it is that I was so normal before my mother died, and I never will be again. I am married to someone I chose because he mothers me and loves me more than anyone I ever knew except my mother. My mother loved me so much, and I thank God that I had ten years with her. That foundation has allowed me to function even in the worst times of my life.

I think the biggest effect my mother's death had on me is my total fear of losing people I love. My poor husband. When he's five minutes late, I'm sure he's had a car accident and more than ten minutes late, I'm planning the funeral. I guess it doesn't help that I also lost my father when I was kind of young (twenty-five) and my first husband when I was thirty-three. Both deaths were devastating—espe-cially my husband's—but *nothing* like losing my mother.

I would have to say my life is much better now as I head fast into forty, but until my midthirties I was a complete mess. I have found my dream job, and my husband started his own business about a year ago and is doing real well. But am I happy? Not really. If I had one wish (besides having my mother back, of course) it would be to be *normal*. All of my friends seem so normal. When I tell them that, they try hard to convince me otherwise, but they never will. I guess I feel that as long as you have your mother, nothing else matters. I will always believe that.

*Chapter Five*

# LIVES SHAPED BY LOSS:
# MORE THAN THIRTY YEARS

By the thirty-year point, a daughter's mourning for her mother involves continually contextualizing the loss, assigning it—and reassigning, when necessary—a meaningful and appropriate place within the larger life story. For many daughters, this involves identifying positive outcomes of early loss. Forty-five-year-old Ilene writes about how the absence of a strong female model gave her the freedom to choose her own path. Seventy-eight-year-old Kate tells her story to classrooms of women to help them create and understand their own personal narratives. Other daughters write of enjoying particularly close relationships with their children, choosing nurturing partners, and devoting themselves to professions that help others cope with loss.

Yet despite these successes, the old feelings of rootlessness and insecurity persist. Our early experiences are the building blocks of the self. They create the foundation for the women we become. When I began sorting through the letters for this chapter, I expected to read only stories of personal victory, as if the insight a motherless woman gained in previous years transforms into a sort of wisdom and peace unique to her. While it's true that the daughters who appear in this chapter seem to have achieved a deeper level of acceptance regarding their losses, we must not confuse acceptance with resignation. What we see in this chapter is a bouquet of women who have learned they can change only the present and the future, not the past. The focus in their letters has shifted away from mother loss and toward the long-term effects a loss has on children who weren't allowed to grieve and who were subjected to a family's secrecy, betrayal, or neglect. As these daughters lead us through the stories of their lives, they show us how the circumstances that precede and follow a mother's death can be, over time, even *more* difficult to reconcile than the loss itself.

Daughters who lost their mothers more than thirty years ago grew up in the households of the 1960s and earlier, in a time when "Don't ask, don't tell" was more than a suggestion—it was a way of life. Their letters describe the overwhelming lack of understanding and support available to girls whose mothers had just died. In this era before the self-awareness movement of the 1970s and the self-help revolution of the 1980s, families typically experienced an emotional shutdown after a trauma, often encouraging the youngest members to act as if the event had never occurred. Recalls forty-six-year-old Charlotte, who was eleven when her mother died of a brain tumor, "My mother was ill for a year and a half. That period of time was excruciatingly painful, as was her death and the months that followed. Those feelings were never discussed, and life in my family was expected to go on 'as usual.'"

Daughters often were left either with grandparents who modeled the pragmatic, detached approach to life and death that served as a psychological defense during the eras of infectious disease, or with traditional fathers of the 1940s, '50s, and '60s who'd typically left the children's emotional care to their wives. Because children will mimic the emotional responses of their surviving caregivers after a mother dies, most daughters in these families tried to suppress or deny their intense feelings of sadness, anger, and despair. But as many of them discovered in later years, grief cannot be avoided—only postponed. Fifty-one-year-old Julia, who was ten and away at boarding school when her mother died, did not attend the funeral and was never encouraged to talk about her mother. Thirty-nine years later, when she reached her mother's age at time of death, she had an intense physical response that sent her into the care of a doctor and a counselor who helped her grieve for a mother who'd died more than three decades earlier.

Julia was fortunate to have found professionals to help her dismantle the wall that had separated her from her grief. Many daughters who do not receive good substitute mothering after a mother's death and do not have the opportunity to express their feelings and mourn become what Dr. Vamik Volkan, the author of *Life after Loss*, calls "perennial mourners." They're always longing, always hoping, always searching for the idealized mother figure who will erase their troubles and make them feel whole.

As I've traveled throughout the United States, Canada, and Britain speaking about *Motherless Daughters* and the long-term effects of early bereavement, I have tried to stress one point whenever possible: We must help young daughters—and sons—*at the time of loss*. More than 125,000 children under the age of eighteen lose their mothers each year just in the United States, a figure that will only increase as AIDS continues to take young mothers from their families. To cope with this growing social crisis, hospitals need more health-care professionals trained to work with families as a whole; local bereavement programs need empathetic volunteers; and children need the support of compassionate relatives, teachers, family friends, and neighbors. We need to work together to create an open, honest approach to mother loss so that girls who are losing their mothers today will look back in another thirty years and tell us stories of triumph, and of being helped through their confusion and pain.

. . .

## SANDY,

*fifty, whose mother died of cancer thirty-one years ago*

I was nineteen when my mother died, and these past thirty-one years have seen me develop into a (sometimes!) mature, capable woman who has many professional responsibilities. Yet the child in me still yearns for my mother's protectiveness, her love, her loyalty, and the woman-to-woman friendship which never fully developed because of the horrible and devastating cancer which robbed her of life when she was only fifty (my age now).

Her presence was so needed and so missed throughout these many years. I was married at age twenty-one, and how empty I felt without her beside me with her praise and pride. When I divorced three years later, I needed her to tell me I would be okay and life would turn out happy even though I was young and divorced.

When I became proficient in my career and started on the road to some success, how much I needed her to encourage me to continue to work even harder so that I could attain any goal that I aspired to.

And in times of crises, such as during a serious operation I had a few years ago, how I yearned for her warmth and care and emotional help and even just being able to say, "Mommy, it hurts," and, "Mommy, I'm scared!"

Yet through these almost thirty-one years, I have grown and matured and, possibly and hopefully, become the woman my mother was at this very age— what a compliment that is to me to think of myself as everything that she was!

And how it seems now that I so easily bond with other motherless daughters and what a special and loving friendship I have with my young friend Robin, who lost her beautiful fifty-eight-year-old mother when she was only thirty. Robin understands. She hurts as I do, and has allowed me to express my feelings, which previously lived only inside me.

### ABBY,
*forty-two, whose mother died of breast cancer thirty-two years ago*

I was ten years old when my mother died. I was her first-born of three daughters, and we had always been very close. It was not the first death I faced in my childhood, nor was it the last. Before I was twenty years old, I saw the passing of an uncle, two aunts, and both grandmothers. My mother and two of her sisters all died of cancer in their forties, leaving behind a total of seven daughters (spread across three families) and two sons. We, in some ways, form the basis for a small, controlled study of our own. One surviving aunt stepped in and took on the first set of cousins whose mother died. Those cousins have led the most emotionally stable lives among the three families. However, when their aunt/stepmother died recently at the age of eighty, they insisted upon referring to her as their mother at the funeral. This puzzled me, because it seemed a denial of their birth mother. It was almost as if they wanted to prove that their lives were more normal than they actually were. The other two families have struggled much more obviously and outwardly with our mothers' deaths and the changes that resulted. In my case, there never was a stepmother, but in the other family of cousins there was a quick remarriage to a woman who was extremely different from the rest of our family.

The year my mom died, I was invited to take her place beside my dad at a family gathering for parents only. I'm sure no one realized what a powerful burden that placed upon my eleven-year-old shoulders. I would say that my mother's death ties for first place as the major influence upon my life. The other one is my relationship with my father.

An aunt once remarked that something in my father died with my mother. I think she was right. For years he was very fragile emotionally, and I remember the scary feeling that he might snap suddenly without warning, but counseling was not an option he chose for himself or for any of us—although I have subsequently chosen it during several difficult periods of my adult life. Instead, he carried his pain deep within. On rare occasions he would burst into tears when he mentioned her name, or his unusually calm temperament would transform into a rage out of proportion to our behavior. All of this was disconcerting to me.

As the second of four brothers, my father knew little about raising daughters. He also knew very little about running a household. He hired a series of live-in housekeepers, all of whom we resented greatly. The first was a woman named Mrs. Roberts with a big German shepherd. Only the dog was allowed to come into our house through the front door. Mrs. Roberts threw all of our toys away while we were at my aunt's house for the week after the funeral, and when we returned, all of the neighborhood children had mysteriously acquired our toys on garbage day. Our next housekeeper had a young daughter who fought viciously with my sisters and slandered my father when he tried to intercede. It went on and on.

Within a couple of years my sister and I had taken over all of the household chores—shopping, cooking, cleaning, washing. It was far better than either my father's attempts or the parade of unloving women who invaded our home. We became highly competent homemakers, always reminding our father to sit back and let *us* take care of things. We saw him as far less than competent at domestics, and for good reason. An old friend of mine still remembers my father sponging up a table spill with his shaving brush. He also washed his dinner dishes in the bathroom sink so that he could dump table scraps down the toilet to avoid clogging the sink drain. The bathroom he knew about, but the kitchen he didn't. Engineering, romping around with us on the carpet, and bedtime stories were his area of expertise. Hugs and intimate conversation and all the subtleties of mothering were foreign territory. I grew up feeling responsible for my father's and my sisters' well-being, yet many of my own basic needs were not being met. This took its toll on me in later years.

I grew up feeling highly competent but insecure, outwardly silly but inwardly serious, extremely mature for my age but completely naive about certain basic social skills. I frequently felt on the fringe of social groups. My sisters and I shared an intense relationship that combined parenting each other with the usual antics of sibling games and rivalry. I saw myself always as somehow more gifted than most children because I had insight into the importance of life and health. I took long walks alone on the beach and wrote deep poetry. I had the feeling a death was hovering around the corner. At one point I even had a formula for how frequently a death in our extended family would occur. On the outside there was joy and laughter and strength. On the inside was sadness, fear, and vulnerability.

Although I had lots of flirtations, I didn't have a steady relationship until I was twenty-one. It was a healthy relationship in many ways, yet I couldn't move beyond a point in terms of commitment. This relationship lingered for years, even after we moved to separate towns and began seeing others. Then I fell into a long-standing pattern of entering relationships that were going nowhere in the long run.

It took my father's death when I was thirty-four to really snap me into completing the grief process. Several weeks before my father's sudden death from a long-term illness for which he had never been hospitalized, I collapsed at a party after a few sips of wine. I woke up in a state of constant panic, from which I did not emerge until months after my father's death. I had lived hundreds of miles from home for years and had traveled extensively on my own, and I was not particularly the greatest at keeping in touch with my dad, but I believe that the deep psychic bond between us was pulled as his death approached, causing my physical and emotional reactions. Though neither of us was totally conscious of it, we had formed a powerful connection that went beyond words and miles. Even the doctors who tested me after the bizarre sequence of physical events confirmed this belief, citing numerous similar examples they had seen in their careers.

My father's death triggered the grief process that had not been completed after my mother's death twenty-four years earlier, even though I had worked on it in counseling and journaling for years. It suddenly hit me so strongly that I wanted a life of my own beyond my connection to my parents, and that I needed to let out all the pain of the past in order to have this. Although I had not been one to shed many tears in the past, I now cried for hours each day. I was so distraught that I had to stop working for a number of months. Much of the year following my father's death was spent grieving the loss of my mother.

At the end of that year I felt a renewed sense of self. I moved in with my sister and returned to graduate school. My sister and I supported each other through the grieving we had left to do. I received a departmental award when I completed my master's degree. At the end of the year I moved into an apartment of my own and began teaching at a couple of colleges in a nearby city. Within a couple of months I met the man who is now my husband.

I married late, at age forty. I have never had children, though I now have two wonderful step-sons. I have always felt ambivalent about having my own children. But I feel that I am coming into a new sense of self, looking for other ways to be a creative and fulfilled person. This growth is, in part, spurred on as I approach the age my mother was at the time of her death, forty-four. I want to envision possibilities for myself that she never knew. And the closer I get to her age, the clearer it becomes to me that we each were given our own paths to walk in life. Believing in this gives me huge amounts of freedom and joy.

## LEIGH,

*forty-four, whose mother died of cancer thirty-two years ago*

I am forty-four years old and twice divorced. When I was twelve years old, my mother died of cancer. Early on, I was held up as an example by my friends' mothers, that is, "My Susie won't even make her bed, but look at Leigh—she's the same age and running an entire household!" While this was initially flattering, soon enough I became aware of the guilt trips and subsequent resentments involved. Even as an adult, I am aware of being exempt from the emotional ambiguity so many women feel toward their mothers. I don't have the unwanted advice (and only a couple of guilt-induced "shoulds") that so many of my friends receive daily from their mothers. Women I know often voice their feelings of resentment or horror at "becoming my mother." So the good news is that I am only becoming me . . .

However, neither have I had the opportunity to thank my mother for the characteristics I gained from her. I admire her sense of adventure: she bought her first convertible once she realized her cancer was terminal. (I own a high-performance car.) She required my brothers and me to taste all foods once (raw oysters at age six!); beyond that, we didn't *have* to eat anything. As an adult, I am still an adventurous eater, yet marvel at how many people never try new or exotic foods. My adventures have also involved corporate and entrepreneurial achievements people told me could not be done; I think my mother would be proud of these.

I remember my mother outlining birth control options to me close to the time she told me she was going to die (I was nine). Much later I realized how the absence of contraceptive options impacted her life, and that she must have wanted different choices available to me. She was ahead of her time in that, and I'm incredibly grateful for her wisdom, vision, and caring. My mother was a talented painter and craftswoman; quilting has become a passion for me in recent years, and I wish she could see how good I'm becoming.

I never got the chance to discuss my parents' relationship with my mother, to get her side of the detrimental compromises I think she made, and to expand her awareness of having more options than she probably perceived. I would have liked to hear her views and to have her see me as a model of emotional, financial, and psychological self-care. Perhaps I would have learned more about what is very nebulous to me, that balance between compromising for a loving relationship and giving up one's self to keep a man's presence or attention. I'm very happy with my life, yet clearly realize I've always chosen to take care of me rather than compromise too much, a likely response to what I saw my mother doing. So perhaps I'm avoiding becoming my mother after all.


NICOLE,
*forty-one, whose mother died of kidney failure thirty-three years ago*

My entire life has been colored by my mother's death when I was eight. My choices at every developmental stage were affected. As I've grown older, I understand more but do not seem to be able to feel less. My choices of romantic partners, my choice of husband, my choice of friends (I prefer people who have been "wounded," who understand pain and, therefore, are more empathetic and human), my decision first not to have children, then to have a child, and then not to have more children are all determined and affected by my mother's early death.

For years I assertively did not want to marry or have children, and chose men to fit that profile—and then was hurt by the limits of their emotional response and commitment. The man I finally married comes from the Iroquois Indian Nation. They are matrilineal—I do not think this is coincidental.

At first, I aggressively avoided becoming a mother. I could not face feeling a child's pain again. I'd had enough pain as a child. Interestingly, feeling the pains of motherhood—the ordinary stuff, as well as being able to *give* unconditional love—has been very therapeutic and cathartic. I am a very overprotective mother, but my mother was, too. I am a very "huggy" mother. I tell my son "be careful" and "I love you" more than I say anything else.

When I gave birth to my son, I lost a lot of blood and my blood pressure fell dangerously low. The nurses told me, "We almost lost you." Though I'd like to have more children, I cannot face the possibility of leaving my son motherless. Today I have a small, enlarged lymph node under my arm. I've had two of these removed elsewhere—totally benign. I have a doctor's appointment scheduled and am sure everything will be fine. I do not fear death or pain, but I do feel I *cannot* die while my son is a child. It is the worst possible thing I can imagine. I know of nothing I could say or do for him now (he is seven) to prepare him for or help him face such a loss.

My own attitude toward separation and loss is terrible. It constantly surprises me. When we moved across the country last year, my husband had to leave a month and a half before my son and I did— at my urging. Yet I felt abandoned and, well, frankly, crazed. Irrational. Understanding this did not soothe the *feeling*. A cat's death, a friend's withdrawal, moving—any loss makes me grieve again as if my mother had died, to a degree greater than it merits.

My entire creative life is centered upon the loss of my mother. I'm a writer, and most of my short stories are what I flippantly call "dead mother stories." I need to be flippant to say anything about it. Unless I am glib about it, I cannot talk about it, but I can write about it and this helps. In stories, I am allowed to feel the loss safely.

EMILY,
*thirty-three, whose mother abandoned her when Emily was an infant*

My older sister, by seventeen months, and I grew up with our father's parents. My grandparents adopted us at the ages of seven and eight, respectively, since we lived with them. This was always odd to me because my father, mother, and three other siblings lived together some sixty-five miles away. I often asked why my sister and I did not live with our parents, but it was quickly explained that my grandparents wanted us to live with them.

When I was seven, my uncle presented me with a picture of a woman with black hair. He told me she was my mother and that her name was Louise. Assuring him that my mother had blonde hair, I told him that it was not true. When my grandmother returned home from work, I asked her about it. She explained that my uncle, her brother, was a mean old man and not to pay any attention to him. Doubt, fear, and many questions began to circulate through my head, but I did not say any more.

At age thirteen, as I thumbed through my grandmother's family Bible, I noticed the marriage year for my parents: 1963. "How could this be?" I thought. "I was born in 1961 and my sister in 1959." I asked about this, and my grandmother explained that it was an error. I knew she had to be lying. She wouldn't make that kind of mistake in her Bible. Knowing that my grandmother had a box on the top shelf of her closet, I waited until I was alone in the house and pulled it down. Inside that big box I found my original birth certificate naming my dad as my father and someone by the name of Louise Jane Wright as my mother, not Maryann, as I had been told. Also in that box I found another birth certificate that named my grandparents as my mother and father as a result of the adoption. Frightened, I quickly replaced all of the items in the box and returned it to its proper place on the shelf. I was overwhelmed by confusion and fear, and questions began filling my head: Who could I talk to about this discovery? What should I tell my sister? Who am I? I had never been so unsure of anything as I was of my identity at that moment.

A few months after my discovery, I went to visit with my father at his home. He and I were alone one afternoon, and I walked into the den where he was watching TV. Point-blank, I asked him if Maryann was my mother. He bolted up off the couch and his six-foot, 280-pound frame loomed over me. In a very deep and vicious voice he said, *"No, and don't you ever mention that to me again!"* Horrified, I ran to the phone and called my grandparents to come and get me. I never went to my father's house alone again after that day, and for three years I did not say a word to anyone in the immediate family about what I found that day. I slowly began to pull away from my family and spent more and more time alone.

My grandfather had been diagnosed with cancer, and when I was sixteen, he was hospitalized. My father's oldest sister and I went to the hospital snack bar, and as we sat there, I stared at my sandwich, trying to gain enough courage to ask her who this Louise person was. Finally I just blurted out, "I know that Maryann is not my mother and that someone named Louise is. Who is she and where is she?" My aunt nearly choked. She began to shake and chain-smoke. After what felt like hours, she slowly began to explain that my mother left the family when I was two and a half months old and my sister nineteen months old. "She just up and left and never came back," was how she described it. She told me that my sister and I were better off not knowing about our mother, but if we ever wanted to find her, she would help us.

Can you imagine the devastation that had just taken place in my life? How could they have hidden this from me? How could they have had Maryann masquerade as my mother when she wasn't, and why wouldn't they talk about it? It was as if Louise being my mother was some big crime that needed to be concealed. Didn't they know that at some point the cover would be blown? I guess they didn't think that it would happen.

My father and I have never been even remotely close. He moved away with his wife, started a new family, and pretended that my sister and I did not exist. Even though he came to visit every month, he never spent time with us. He always went fishing, watched football on TV, or did whatever else he wanted. On Sunday, he and his family would load up in the car and head back to their home.

I went through a number of romances as a teen-ager and young adult with men five to twenty years older than myself. Part of me was searching for a father figure and the other part—I'm not sure. I sup-pose I just wanted to be close to a male. I wanted to be taken care of, made to feel secure and loved. When I met my husband, I knew that I had finally found the kind of man that I had been searching for. His family has become the kind of family that I wanted to be a part of while growing up. His parents have taken me in and treat me as one of their own children. My father-in-law comes to see me every day and talks to me just like one of his daughters. The "other" daughter-in-law does not have the kind of relationship that I do with my in-laws.

As I was planning my wedding, I wanted my mother for the first time. I needed her to be there with me while all of the preparations were under way. I had no idea what I was supposed to be doing, but thank God for my mother-in-law. She kept me straight on all of the formalities of wedding plans.

When my first child was born, those same feelings of longing returned, only stronger. As I held my daughter for the first time and looked down into her tiny face, my heart began to break. How could my mother experience what I just went through giving birth and walk out of my life—never to return? I think (and I say this because I have nothing to compare it to) that it's harder to be abandoned by your mother than to have her die. Death is final, and you know in your heart and soul that your mother is never coming back. When she just leaves, you always have that hope that one day you will be reunited.

Someone once told me that when I became secure in my life, I would seek out my mother. I guess that's what happened two years ago. Five days before my thirty-first birthday, I called my aunt and told her I wanted a name of some family member of my mother's. She gave me a last name and a town. I pulled down the telephone directory and began calling Wrights in the phone book. After two tries, I reached my mother's uncle. I asked him to be patient with me while I explained who I was and who I was looking for. He was shocked. He had not seen my mother in twenty-five years, but he had her address and phone number across the country. He called and told her that I had contacted him and that if she was willing, I wanted to talk with her. I had prepared myself for the worst: that she did not want to talk to me. My uncle called me back in less than ten minutes and said she was waiting by her phone. I took a deep breath and dialed her number. With me on the phone and my husband on the extension, we talked coast to coast for almost two hours. She tried to explain some things to me, and I tried to understand. We hung up with promises to keep in touch. Over the next year, we spoke every month and mailed cards and pictures. For the first time that I can remember, I saw a photograph of my mother. What a strange feeling, to look for the first time at a picture of the woman who gave birth to you—a luxury most daughters take for granted.

In April of the following year, my mother telephoned to say that she was going to be on the East Coast in June. She wanted me to come to see her, if possible. Two months later, my husband and I set out by car for the seven-and-a-half-hour journey. I was terrified. As we crossed a bridge ten miles from our home, I looked out across the water. I knew that the next time I crossed that bridge, I would not be the same person that I was at that very moment.

We arrived on schedule and checked into the motel where my mother and her husband were staying. We met in my room and talked for hours. So many emotions ran through me the moment I opened the door and we stood face to face. We both felt good to see each other, but I came away from the trip both physically and mentally exhausted. All I wanted to do was to get home to my children and familiar surroundings. I cried the first two hours on the return trip home, not because I was sad that we were separating again but because all of my childhood fantasies were now gone. All of the dreams about her had been shattered by reality, and I needed some time to deal with that. My husband has been incredibly supportive, as has his family. I could not have undertaken this mission without them.

My family, on the other hand, has been less than enthused. My sister has so much bitterness about the situation that we cannot discuss our mother. We were never close growing up and remain distant today. My grandmother was furious that I wanted to find Louise. She felt betrayed that she had taken me in and raised me and then I turned on her by seeking out my birth mother. I've never discussed with my father finding Louise or seeing her. The funny thing about my dad is that he can't figure out why he and I have never had any type of relationship. (Maybe it has to do with the fact that not only did my mother abandon me but he did, too.) My sister and I are a reminder of a past he doesn't want to remember. I suppose my mother leaving him hurt so much that he had to bury his feelings.

At times I feel like an orphan. My grandparents did the best they could raising us, but they never took the place of "real" parents. My grandfather never raised his voice, but we called my grandmother "the warden" while we were growing up. She was (and still is) very controlling and a strict disciplinarian.

As far as how I have managed, the answer is, okay. I have a tendency to be very independent. I grew up having to solve my own problems because Grandmother did not want to be bothered or the generation gap was too wide. I still have problems asking others for help. I would rather take care of a situation myself than have to ask for assistance. I grew up in a home where emotions were not shown and where I was constantly talked down to. I was and still am an insecure person. As a parent, I find myself repeating the same behaviors that Grandmother exhibited: not being affectionate, isolating myself, not showing emotion except for anger, and being too businesslike. Another mother recently told me that I run my house like a military post. Boy, what a reality slap! I have begun to make a conscious effort to be more "motherly." (I do the best I can, having had a poor example set for me when I was growing up.)

The section in *Motherless Daughters* about "Love Substitutes" describes me more than I like to admit. I use overspending as a method to feel good about myself. As an overachiever, I have recently started attending college and maintain a 4.0. I use my academic work as a source of positive feedback. The encouragement and support that my professors give me reinforce my need to feel valuable. Not that being a wife and mother isn't important, but I need something more. I have to stay busy. If I sit around and have too much idle time, I can't deal with all of the pain still inside of me. I feel afraid, but I don't know of what. Does that make sense to you?

Although I did not experience the death of my mother, in an odd way her absence could be viewed as a death. She was missing from the family picture, and no one wanted to talk about her. I suppose for all practical purposes, she was dead. I, too, have had to do some mourning for the loss of my dreams about her. I spent some time in therapy trying to put all of my behavior patterns into some kind of order. During one session we had a mock funeral for the "dream mother." I had no idea how difficult that mourning would be. I've survived, battered but intact.

I still have a long way to go with putting all of my past behind me, but my prayer is that one day I can lead a full life and be the person that I want to be.

# ILENE,

*forty-four, whose mother died of heart failure thirty-five years ago*

I began my journey into my loss and my past twelve years ago, and I was never so scared as I was the day my pastor went with me to meet the counselor I had chosen. I entered treatment because I felt my life was falling apart, and I couldn't stop it. I was having severe anxiety attacks, I felt like I was always being talked about, and I felt ugly and didn't like myself. I had been through a job loss that crippled my career. My father had died of cancer, and I had two children, with no parent to talk with about raising them. I felt so alone, even though I was married. I even felt suicidal at times because the pain was so great. I read and read, but couldn't find anything that could explain what was wrong with me and why I felt so alone.

The first year of therapy, which was only two sessions a month, was spent analyzing. My counselor would listen to me, and we would discuss in detail why I did this or that. When I realized I was getting nowhere, she explained that all I did was analyze and that I needed to learn more about feelings. I had to do a series of exercises to explore the sadness that was inside me. Once I accepted those feelings, I discovered I was terribly depressed due to the loss of my mother when I was nine. With my therapist's help, I began to delve into the loss and discovered how it had affected me. I also discovered that I had never grieved for her. I was always the little soldier who tried to keep everyone happy and forgot about myself. I had to work through a lot of memories of feeling alone, times when I had no safety net to fall into. As a child, I had to deal with events that a child can't handle alone, and no one was there to say, "It's okay," or, "I'm here for you."

I realized the other day when visiting with another motherless daughter that my desire to run away and my persistent fear that everyone was talking about me came from after my mother died. When I entered a room, all the mothers would look at me and whisper to each other about the little girl without a mother. I felt like an oddity in the community, because it was a small town and mother loss was not common. The women didn't mean to be cruel, but when no one talks to you and instead people whisper about you, it makes you feel like a freak. Just the other day a woman who had been a good friend of my parents told me about the day of my mom's funeral. She said I was sitting in a big chair all alone and kept looking at her with big eyes. She said she always wished she had asked my father if I could sit with her, but she said at that time you just didn't do that. She said she didn't want to make me feel sad, but she wanted me to know this. I

thought this was nice of her and told her that although I don't remember that scene, I'm sure I was a
very lost little girl that day.

There are times when I feel alone, but not as
much now that I understand where it comes from. I
have two wonderful children, and I communicate
with them as much as possible. I know how important it is to be a good parent and to make them feel
good about themselves. I always felt like the odd
person out, the one who didn't fit in anywhere. I was
always trying to get approval and to be liked, and I
never stuck up for myself, because no one ever
taught me that I was important. Now I feel that I
count and that I have a lot to contribute. I don't let
people tell me how I feel or how I should think. I
have become a doer rather than a follower, hoping
to change what I feel needs to be changed. Not having a mother for a model has allowed me to become
my own person, even though it has taken me forty-
five years.

## MADELYN,
*forty-seven, whose mother died in a fire forty years ago*

My mother died in a fire that destroyed our home
when I was seven years old. My father and my six-
year-old brother and I survived. I was burned much

worse than they were, and spent about a year in the hospital. I have scars on my body still. Strangely enough, even though I have these scars, I have been called beautiful, striking, and attractive for reasons I have never really understood myself.

I have few memories of my mother, but when I think of her, I remember that it was she who came to my room and wrapped me in a sheet and carried me down a burning staircase and handed me to my father, who put me out on the front lawn with my brother. I have heard people say that she returned to the house, perhaps to save something. I remember that I cried to my father when he went into the house after her, "Don't go—Mother's gone."

My father and brother went to live in my aunt and uncle's house, and I joined them when I got out of the hospital. I had a nurse for a while, but I don't remember much about her. After she left, my cousin Trudi came to live with us, also at Aunt and Uncle's. I suppose she was in her twenties then, and she was to look after us. Trudi was the best thing that could have happened to us except for Aunt and Uncle. Or, rather, all of them made possible for us as normal a life as possible under the circumstances.

I don't remember too much of my father during that time, although I know from pictures I have of us that he read to us and took us to the country during that period. He had another house built, and after about two years we moved—me, my brother, Trudi, and Daddy. I guess our life was normal. Most every memory I have of that time is of the beach, Brownies and Boy Scouts, and trips Trudi took us on. She was strict but fun—we did not feel unloved.

My mother must have had a lot of friends, and to this day people tell me about her. They say she was a beauty, and in her pictures she is pretty, but mostly they talk about how generous she was. She always organized the parties and projects for children at our school. Her best friend tells me the story of when Mother and Father were looking for an old house to buy and restore and found one owned by two older women in the country. They couldn't afford to keep it up, but when Mother met them, she felt so sorry for them she had my father arrange to have the house fixed up for them to continue living in instead.

My maternal grandmother lived until 1978. My mother's death was very hard on her. She told me that my mother told her one afternoon that she thought she was not going to live much longer and that she was worried about what would happen to me and my brother.

I remember very well the day my father took us to visit a woman at her parents' house. I also remember one night in the den when he told us he was considering getting married—and I said, "We want you to be happy, Daddy."

We were told Trudi was leaving to go home, and

my brother and I were sent to summer camp for three weeks. When we came home, Gloria, our new stepmother, was there. We were nine and ten years old then. I guess we assumed life would go on as normal, with just a "new" Trudi. Instead, it was the beginning of a special kind of hell: my grandmother was not allowed to visit us at our house; most of the time when we got home from school, Gloria would be in her room with her mother visiting her; one day in her car, Gloria told me we should be nicer to our father because he didn't have to keep us.

Gloria was and is a very cold person. Now, as an adult, I can say she was a vicious, jealous, greedy creature.

She left my brother alone, mostly. However, it seems I could do nothing right, and I began to be punished physically, mostly by being slapped in the face.

At some point my father began to start the same treatment toward me. Once I spoke up and said something about Gloria not being fair, and my father slapped me repeatedly, time after time with both hands until finally I started screaming. I remember him stopping and saying to himself, "What have I done?" over and over.

As I got older, this changed somewhat. First my father took my brother and me aside one Sunday morning and told us we were adopted but that only meant we were really wanted. Then, later, Gloria and Daddy told us Gloria was going to have a baby.

After their son was born, Gloria mostly left us alone, but we weren't allowed around our half-brother at all. Our bedrooms were upstairs, and Gloria had an extra room turned into a den. That is where my brother and I spent most of our time. We got plates and ate upstairs alone most of the time.

One strange thing happened that I have never forgotten. My father accosted me one morning demanding to know what I had been doing. It seems some "serviceman" had written me a letter. I was about fourteen then and frankly was a tomboy. Almost every free moment of my life was spent at the stable with horses. I didn't know any serviceman or even anyone outside our town. I asked to see the letter, and Father said Gloria had destroyed it. My father was accusing me of something I didn't even have an understanding of. I believe, and always will, that my stepmother made this up or created the scene.

It was strange—being afraid and angry and helpless, yet even at that age I was outraged at the injustice. Finally, in the eleventh grade I was sent away to school, and then I went to college and then to work and then to marriage and then to divorce and then to the real work world. I hardly ever saw Gloria or Daddy once I went away to school. They had another son and built another house.

On my honeymoon, my father called me and asked if I told my husband what a bad father he was. I loved my husband, but I drove him away, I believe, with the hidden anger and impossible requirement that he make up for the love I never had. This is my biggest regret.

Once, after I divorced, I visited my father's office to store some papers there. In a file marked "Family Corresp." I saw a letter he had written to business associates when I was in college in another state. It said he would appreciate them checking on me since I had "problems" but that it was not necessary that they have me in their homes.

It was then, I believe, that I let go of my father—not let go of the past, but let go of hope—and although he died in 1989, I think that as my "daddy" he died then for me, when I saw a man so weak he would use the reputation of a child to cover up the sickness of his wife.

My brother and I have been close off and on, but he has a family and lives in another state now. The last time I saw him was at Father's funeral. Neither he nor I were mentioned in his will, and although we did not expect to inherit anything, it was strange not to have ever heard from his executor. It wasn't an emotional feeling, really, just more like feeling. Isn't it odd how people can change a life or hurt a life just by wishing you away?

Now I am forty-seven. I have decided that love

is loyalty and true concern for another's quality of life and well-being. I have done some good for some people—I have probably hurt some—I could have been worse—but then I could have been happier.

If it seems this is not about Mother, it is. One thing I have thought about for all these years is the day a woman came to interview me because Gloria was to adopt us formally. To her questions I said yes or whatever I was supposed to say, because I was afraid. But what I wanted to say was, "No, no, no." I had to get a new birth certificate for a trip, and when I saw Gloria's name listed as my mother, I felt sick.

I am having a hard enough time as it is making a living, but every week I think as soon as I can afford the legal fees I am going to find a way to undo that adoption, if it is the last thing I ever do.

At my father's funeral, after everyone left, I slid a snapshot of my mother into the crack of the lid of his coffin—for the man he was when he was with her, and for her.

Someone asked me recently if I get lonely, and I said to myself, "So what? I've been lonely all my life." Even if I had not gone through the abuse from my stepmother, I think I would still have that corner of lonely, maybe not so big but still there. My mother loved us; she saved me. But there was no time for her to see me become a person and love me, good or bad, right or wrong, always. A mother is always there for you, and if you have enough time for memories, she is always with you, even when she is gone.

My cousin Trudi, who knew we were adopted, asked me once if I was curious about who my real parents were. Perhaps I am not normal to not wonder or not care.

I had a real mother. My mother. Her name was Rose. She died in a fire after saving her children on February 5, 1951.


## MARY,

*fifty-six, whose mother died after a second stroke forty years ago*

I'm the fourth in a family of five with three older brothers and a younger sister. Our father died of a heart attack when I was five years old, so I have no memories of him as a person. My mother was my sole security and friend as a young girl, but when I was fourteen years old, she suffered a stroke and had to be in the hospital for ten weeks, at which time I became the mother of our family, since I was the oldest daughter. Upon her recovery, she asked me to travel to Great Britain with her for five weeks to tour, in spite of the brace on her left leg, the cane she used for walking, and the limited use of her left arm. She knew this would be her last trip, and to spend this personal time with her alone and celebrate my sixteenth birthday there is an experience I have never forgotten.

The following year I could see her losing her capabilities, and I was living with the fact that a second stroke would probably be fatal. She died a month before I graduated from high school. My plan was to continue on to college that fall and keep busy, which I have done up until five years ago with marriage and raising two wonderful children. My time to mourn and grieve had been suppressed for thirty-five years until the children left home for college and now marriage. I was embracing my relationship with my daughter for many years with high hopes that I could find that bond in my life, but now with her marriage in April and a permanent move to Europe I awake to the truth that nothing can ever replace that loss. Through many moments of tears, wanting so badly to share my life with my mother and still seeking her guidance, I'm realizing I must learn to live with the loss.

I recently became determined to eradicate a stress-related condition I've suffered from all my life. I've been taking massage therapy once a week for three years now. I've given myself this personal time to heal my body, and not only have I seen incredibly physical results, but I've also seen this death which I had suppressed finally come forth to be cared for. I allowed the tears to flow whenever the sadness came over me. Picking wildflowers for our home, having my daughter living so far away, my son taking a wife, losses taking place in my life, just seem to make me cry even harder, wishing I could be comforted by my mother. I yearn from this need, but my husband doesn't seem to know how to fill it for me, nor does anyone except my brother, who is two years older than I am. He seems to be the one who understands most. He gives me praise and guidance and is the one person in my life who always says at the end of a visit or phone call, "I love you, Mary." It's truly music to my ears and always brings the tears.

To continue my healing process, I went a step further and started meditation, practicing this discipline twice a day, and absolute miracles have happened in my life. Thus I feel I have finally learned how to heal myself from within, but I agree with you, that the loss of my mother is now having a greater effect upon me because of my age. I'm looking back over forty years of my life and seeing all the times when I needed my mother but she wasn't here to be with me. I'm now allowing all these feelings to surface, but I can only hope in due time my outward emotions will quiet down.

## JULIA,

*fifty-one, whose mother died of colon cancer forty-one years ago*

My mother died when I was ten and she was forty-nine. Since my father (himself fatherless since age seven) worked in West Africa, an environment at that time considered too unhealthy for children, my mother had often left us in the care of one or the other grandmother for periods of one or more years. When I was seven, we were sent to a boarding school, like many other English children.

I think my mother developed cancer of the bowel about eighteen months before her death. My father, out of love for my mother, forbade anyone to tell her (and, of course, her children) that she had cancer and that her death was only a matter of time.

This absence of a stable home and the lack of mourning at the time of my mother's death had a major impact on the lives of my older sister and myself.

We were at boarding school when the head mistress, who was very kind, broke the news of my mother's death first to my sister and then to myself. After ten or twenty minutes my sister was sent to finish her homework in the classroom, and I was sent to bed in a single room which was normally considered the "sickroom."

We did not attend my mother's funeral. Why, I don't know. Perhaps because people thought it might upset us! Because I never talked about my mother and could not even say her name for years, I did not know how she died until I was in my early twenties. I never spoke of her or her death to any relatives until I was in my forties. So much for the British stiff upper lip!

By the time I was twenty-four, I had left England and both my grandmothers and my father had died. Four years later, an aunt whom I got to know in my late teens and who was wonderfully supportive died from cancer—a totally unexpected death. Due to distance, I attended none of these funerals.

When I was forty-nine, my mother's age when she died, I had a solitary grand mal seizure. This started a chain of events which has changed my life for the better.

I became aware that I was depressed, started taking courses in creative writing, went to an excellent counselor, and wept copious tears especially on the next anniversary of my mother's death, when I was older than she had ever been.

Mourning for one's mother is such a private process, it is hard to realize we have many fellow travelers. Perhaps a sense of shame for not having the necessary "woman-knowledge" or social skill has kept me more private than necessary. Reading of other women who deal with this lack so openly

helps me understand I do not have to blame myself
for its absence.

## LOUISE,
*fifty-eight, whose mother died forty-three years ago*

I was fifteen when my mother died. Previously, I
knew of a neighbor girl whose father had died, and
that made her almost of a different species, one only
whispered about. We lived only a block away, but it
would never have occurred to me to be friends with
her—she was *different*. Then, when it happened to
me, I joined her company, knowing I had become
one of the whispered-about ones. I can even remember her name forty-three years later, yet I never even
met her in person. She was the only person I knew
of who shared my aura of oddness in high school.

My father, in his grief, denied us ours—"You
girls only lost a mother and you're nearly grown; I
lost my *life partner*!" For the next two years we lived
with his verbal, emotional, and, for my older sister,
physical abuse. Yet we never told anyone, even when
friends asked us if something was wrong at home.
We lied, and then when the friends left, all cried
from shame and fear.

One time when we did call for help (my father
constantly threatened suicide, and purposely took a

drug to which he was violently allergic), the pastor made light of our worries, so we sat up much of the night to listen to his gurgling breathing and, by morning, he was sleeping soundly.

In college, one assignment in child education was to plan parties for the class. One group of girls planned a Mother's Day party. The custom then, in the fifties, was for a woman to wear a colored flower in honor of her mother, or a white one if her mother was dead. My best friend and I each sat in silence with our white roses pinned on, and the rest of the day I was in a state of gloom. We were *different*.

Three years ago my daughter bore our first grandson, and he died shortly after birth. I struggled with my grief for nearly six months, feeling somehow everyone else was going on with life while I was caught in a giant minor chord that never quieted. Finally, I went for counseling, knowing that all my life I had tried and failed to understand what had happened for the two years of my life I described as "horror." In only six intense sessions I went back forty years and put all the puzzle pieces out and faced the unbearable parts. It was the best thing I ever did for myself, and one of the hardest. My daughter, in her grief writings, expressed it this way: "My mother is not able to deal with her grief adequately, and it goes back into the past. When Kyle's life made her a grandmother, she was not able to handle it because she had no matching line extending back into the past. Only when she was able to understand her own past was she able to accept the life and death of her grandson."

Just sharing this brings up the old lump in the throat.

## CHRISTINE,

*sixty-eight, whose mother abandoned her fifty-four years ago*

I am the product of a dysfunctional family—an alcoholic father and a depressed mother who, in turn, had been brought up in her own dysfunctional family. My memory of my mother is of a shadowy figure, often lying in a darkened room with an ice pack on her head. I don't remember her ever laughing, and I can't remember her ever playing with or reading to my sister or myself. Our father did that—when he wasn't drunk. The only time my mother seemed to be there for us was when we were sick. She was a good and conscientious caretaker, and in that she was comforting. However, she wasn't there to hear our stories, our failures and successes, our fears. So eventually I, at least, seemed to come to the conclusion that my very presence was a burden to her.

In the face of this it seemed prudent to be silent

and self-effacing, thereby removing as much of her burden as possible. My sister did that very well. I, on the other hand, felt I had to speak up when I thought something was unjust. And one day our mother left.

Actually, she went to Canada for her father's funeral. That was early in December, and she said she'd be back for Christmas. But she wasn't. She said her stepmother needed her and she'd be back in early January. And then began, for my sister and myself, the agonizing and increasingly less hopeful wait as one deadline after another passed, until my father gave her an ultimatum to return, and at last the fearful hoping was over. Our mother wasn't coming back. We really must have been too much of a burden for her. She hadn't even said good-bye. She never explained. She had been with us constantly for all of my fourteen years, and then she had simply left.

I had always been uneasy speaking up in the presence of more than two or three adults, and now I was *terrified*. I had continued to speak in the face of evidence that to do so was unwise, and the ultimate had happened. I had driven my mother away.

I saw her only once after that—five years after she left us. At that point I was nineteen and wanted nothing to do with her, and my actions made that fairly clear. I always knew where she was living, at her childhood home. When I was thirty-five and less bitter, I wrote to her—twice—asking to hear from her and promising no intrusion into her privacy other than that. The letters were unanswered and unreturned. However, a few years ago I renewed an acquaintance with cousins and children of cousins on my mother's side and found that she had died at about the same time I had written to her, so possibly she never received the letters. In fact, I was told that when my mother died, my cousin called to tell us. She was told by my father's sister, who had been living with us since Mother left, that we were "not interested." We were never told. I also learned that my father beat my mother, which might explain her unwillingness to return, but still . . .

I am sixty-eight years old now, and my life has been darkened by this pervasive sorrow. My career in international relations certainly was diminished by my fear of speaking in groups. I never asked a question at a meeting; I never made a comment; I never seconded a motion. The problem is evident socially as well. Given the fact that six or eight people represent "public" to me and evoke my fear of public speaking does not make me a sought-after dinner party guest.

This problem is an albatross I have lived with, worked around, and eventually started to deal with professionally when such problems acquired a label: phobia. The process has been painful and discouraging, but then, so has my life. But I can see definite progress now. The new medications have helped me tremendously in reducing anxiety. In my experience, they have the potential for cutting years off the therapeutic process.

## BRENDA,
*fifty-seven, whose mother was institutionalized from the time Brenda was an infant*

My mother disappeared from my life when I was only a few months old. She had a postpartum psychosis and was hospitalized in a state mental institution after the treatment offered at that time failed to help her. I have *no* recollection of my mother. What did she look like? What did her voice sound like? Did she love and want me?

My childhood was spent as a very "good little girl" shuttled back and forth between relatives. As a motherless daughter, I learned early in life to be well-behaved, and then hopefully no one would want to send me away. I don't remember anyone *ever* talking about my mother, or offering an explanation of where she was, during my childhood or adolescence. So I just buried my questions, my loss, and my grief.

My mother died in the state hospital when she was forty-nine years old and I was about twenty-one.

I had never been allowed to visit or see her. At the funeral, I felt numb and was not encouraged to mourn or feel the loss.

The first time I remember missing and crying for my mother was when I had my own daughter. I suddenly felt something huge missing from my life. Who would help me and teach me to care for this baby? I felt there was no one I could trust to care for my precious baby girl.

I filled my daughter's life with love but was never able to share with her the story of my loss. Your book has helped me start the process of my own healing, as well as enabling me to *begin* sharing the story of my loss with my daughter. I have hope that even at the "advanced" age of fifty-seven my heart can now find the healing and peace I crave.

FRAN,
*sixty-two, whose mother committed suicide fifty-nine years ago*

I was born into a family of Italian immigrants, and my mother suicided when I was three. There is so much to this story that I have even written a novel, hiding myself in 1855 Italy to try to attach some meaning to my feelings.

My mother's death was a scar on the Italian

Catholic family. I was not told she committed suicide until I was about thirty-five, when my sister
who was ten years older told me when I needed to
know the cause of my mother's death for medical
reasons. Her life and her death became the family
secret. If I asked, I was told not to ask silly questions. My father moved into a hotel and referred to
my mother only as a Madonna. I was placed with my
maternal grandmother. My sister was placed in an
all-girls Catholic school where I had little contact
with her until she was married. She died a very, very
difficult death at fifty-five of obesity. I feel her story
should have been heard, but she learned early not to
ask or tell.

I was not told my mother had died until about
six months after her death. Instead, I was told she
had gone away. Not even any angels or heaven! I
reacted by running to the train station and streetcars,
waiting for her to come home. Not until I was about
fifty-eight did I demand some answers, but still very
little was given to me.

I bore the guilt; it was my fault. I had been very
ill with ear infections and had a mastoid performed
on me. The doctor cut my facial nerve, leaving the
left side of my face paralyzed. As young as I was, I
have memories of my mother crying, trying to make
me pretty again, sitting on the edge of the bathtub as
she curled my hair. My grandmother would tell me I
was a pretty girl if I did not smile.

I felt I never belonged, as if I was simply a boarder and that when I grew up, I was expected to leave. I lived with my sixty-five-year-old grandmother; my sister when her husband went overseas during the war; and then when my mother's perfect sister remarried a wealthy man when I was twelve, I moved in with her . . . but again it was not my home. At one time, as a small child, I fantasized that I would change my name to "I Love You" just so I could hear those words spoken.

All my financial needs were met—none of the emotional. I, too, was sent to Catholic school. What a great substitute for a mother—nuns! I learned to survive by being the good little girl, never letting anyone close to me, and becoming determined that I would grow up and marry a handsome, ambitious man and have four children. I would become the mother that I did not have.

I did marry and have four children. I was often frustrated being a mother, for there was no pattern for me to follow as a mother or a wife. With God on my side, I am very proud to say I have four great children and five perfect grandchildren.

The marriage ended in divorce after thirty-four years. He was first-generation German born, workaholic, alcoholic. That is another story. I entered therapy to deal with the divorce and my anger. I realized that the divorce had very little to do with my anger and the real issue was my family of origin. My mother didn't think me worthwhile and copped out of life. My father chose not to be in my life to fill any emotional needs. My grandmother was too busy cleaning and crying because my grandfather had a series of mistresses. My maternal aunt, very good at providing all the material things I needed, was busy cultivating her role in society. There was no time for me, and I knew that I could not ask.

I did therapy in the Gestalt method and the visualization method, and went to workshops and anything that could help me break through this idea I had that I was not good enough, pretty enough, thin enough, smart enough.

I do believe that somehow my mother still is with me—not in spirit, because I did not know her, but in the children I have borne and the children they have borne. I see actions and hand movements that I don't recognize, and sometimes I think to myself that maybe, just maybe, that look or that action comes from my mother and she somehow lives.

I am what I am because of my life, because of what I have been and done. I still have an issue with trust, but I no longer fear abandonment. I walked through that and I survived. I write. I paint. I am happy with my creativity. I live well, travel, and all in all have learned to love myself as much as I have expected others to love me. But I still wonder, what if?

My mother chose not to live. I have resolved

this. The distorted lies that my family chose to tell me have been the most difficult issue to resolve.

I survived at the time, and that was enough. Now I live because of the life I have created. My wish is that for all motherless daughters.

## KATE,

*seventy-eight, whose mother died two hours after her birth*

I received your book on my seventy-eighth birthday as a gift from a young friend. I quickly scanned it for references to women who lost their mothers at birth, that tragic time of "her life or mine." I started reading and kept right on through to the end, with epiphanies along the way. Losing a mother certainly makes a difference in how a life goes.

My mother bled to death about two hours after I was born. She was seventeen. When I was just past two, my father remarried a woman who had no use for me. I stayed with my maternal grandparents, aunts, uncles, and extended family in a small village of about three hundred, surrounded by cattle ranches.

Today, I tell my life story over and over to women of many different cultures—Polynesian, Asian, Caucasian, and that unique culture of army wives. I started teaching a class called "Women in Transition" in the 1970s, and the responses I get from the women indicate that I have been effective in making my story universal.

I had a childhood memory while working with these classes, an early memory that shook me. I remembered making a promise. I buried my dolls and then dug them up, complete with ritual, promising I would never leave them. I had not told anyone about my forbidden games. I was about four or five.

I married early and pregnant, giving up the scholarship I had won in high school. I enjoyed my three children. They taught me with their enthusiasm and curiosity. Later, at fifty, after I had seen all three married and I thought safe and "secure," I walked away—to another job, another life.

My only daughter died four years ago from complications of a liver disease. She had lived here near me since her "secure" marriage failed. We became friends, good friends, sharing mutual challenges, facing the reality of our early relationship with each other, sharing family secrets. I had never experienced anything like the devastation and pain I felt after her death.

You talk of each loss reminding us of earlier losses. When I read your book, and even as I'm composing this letter, I feel the pain of the loss of a daughter. As I mourn for my daughter, I'm acutely aware of how hard it has been to mourn for a mother who had no skin, and remained ethereal and immortalized.

Aunts and uncles who alternately took care of me and taunted me in turn made comparisons, as they remembered their sister. "You don't look like your mother—you are dark haired, not blonde like her"; and, "Your teeth are coming in crooked; she had straight, even teeth, a great smile"; or, "Your face is freckled like a turkey egg, like your father's was. Her skin was milk white."

None of these comparisons came from Ellen Jean, my strong pioneer grandmother who said nothing and showed me how to survive. Not long ago, I found some pictures, one of me with a friend, and on the back someone had written, "She was cute as a button." I didn't know anyone ever thought that about me.

Anxiety attacks about two years after my daughter's death sent me back to therapy, for more understanding.

One among the many sentences from your book that lifted itself off the page: "But from underneath all the glitz still comes the cry of the motherless child, 'Pay attention to me!'"

The label persists. *I am a motherless child*. When I hear the title of the gospel song, I automatically add the words, "A long way from home."

*Epilogue*

# THE BIRTH OF SUPPORT

All roads may once have led to Rome, but in my past most roads have led from Evanston, Illinois. It was there, as a freshman at Northwestern University, where I began my search for books about early mother loss. And it was there, nine years later, that I decided to write *Motherless Daughters* after the notices I tacked up in a local café and bookstore when I was looking for other motherless women led to more phone calls than I could possibly manage. So it's perfectly appropriate that the first woman who asked me about starting a support group for motherless daughters did so at a reading in downtown Evanston.

I can't recall exactly what she said, and I don't think I ever got her name. But I remember that the sheet of notebook paper she passed around collected about twenty names and telephone numbers from women interested in forming a local group. The same thing happened in St. Paul, Minnesota; and in Atlanta; and Los Angeles; and Portland, Oregon; and New York. "I came here tonight so I could sit in a room with other women like myself after years of feeling so alone," a woman in San Diego said. "But tonight isn't enough. I want to do it again and again and again."

As these women had learned, breaking through the wall and shame of silence that surrounds many motherless daughters would be only the first step toward coming to terms with their pasts. Yes, it's essential to begin talking about our losses, but we need people to talk *with*.

When I started writing *Motherless Daughters*, I'd never spoken with another motherless woman to any real depth, yet the ones I've met over the past two years have become my most valuable source of comfort and support. They're the women who can tell me what it's like to mother a daughter when you haven't had that relationship for so long, and how it feels to live beyond the age a mother was when she died. They understand my doubts and fears more intimately than any of my other female friends possibly could.

With this in mind, on August 30, 1994, six women who'd lost their mothers during childhood, adolescence, and early adulthood sat down in a Greenwich Village restaurant to plan the first Motherless Daughters Support Groups. We began with a blank notebook, a pencil, and a total of ninety-eight years' worth of experience as motherless women. As we went around the table, each woman offered what she envisioned as a goal for the groups: To provide motherless women with a sense of community. To offer a safe, supportive environment for the free expression of feelings. To validate a daughter's experiences, both positive and negative.

We decided the groups would meet one evening a week for ten weeks; be closed meetings limited to ten women or fewer so that all members would have ample time to speak and be heard; focus on one topic per week, with an overall structure loosely related to the chapters in *Motherless Daughters*; and be led by a facilitator trained in group leadership. From the start, we determined that these groups would be support groups, not therapy groups. We strongly urge that women rely on such groups as an adjunct to professional counseling rather than as a substitute for it.

Our first two trial groups ran in New York City from mid-September until late December. In February we began another cycle with four groups meeting in Manhattan. Growth has been slow, but steady. We have wanted time to listen to women's feedback and modify the groups to best suit their needs.

Our first facilitator was a certified social worker who lost her mother at age thirteen and volunteered to help us get started. Our group leaders are now graduates of the ten-week program who attended our special Motherless Daughters workshop in leadership and group dynamics. Although I'm in favor of groups for motherless women starting in other cities, I stress the importance of a leader who understands how to cope with uncomfortable situations. If five motherless women in Denver want to meet for coffee once a week to share stories about their mothers, fine. But if those same five women want to discuss all the anger, guilt, sadness, and pain that came with early mother loss, I can guarantee there will be evenings when raw and potentially volatile emotions enter the room. I've heard stories from women who quite benevolently tried to start groups in their hometowns, only to watch their best intentions dissolve into a fiery session of father-bashing that sent women home in tears. The responsibility issues are enormous when someone's psychological health is at stake. A well-defined group structure and a facilitator with personal experience in a similar group, plus some training in group leadership, are essential.

At the moment, I suggest that motherless women in other cities who wish to start support groups find a local therapist with an interest in mother-daughter issues—ideally, one who's motherless herself—who's willing to lead such a group for an affordable fee. The new Motherless Daughters nonprofit organization in New York plans to continue to offer groups in New York and has expanded the program to six other cities in the U.S. and Canada. We're also publishing a Motherless Daughters newsletter to connect women nationwide. As daughters who've lost our mothers, we are already bound by our common experience. By sharing that experience with the members of our informal sorority, we hope to find additional solace in each other's words.

For more information about joining Motherless Daughters and subscribing to the newsletter, please send a SASE to:

Motherless Daughters
Cherokee Station
Box 20710
New York, NY 10021-0074

Please allow four to six weeks for delivery.

# Sources and Resources

Cole, Diane. *After Great Pain: A New Life Emerges*. New York: Summit, 1992.

De Beauvoir, Simone. *A Very Easy Death*. New York: Pantheon, 1985.

Ernaux, Annie. *A Woman's Story*. New York: Ballantine, 1992.

Kaplan, Louise J. *No Voice Is Ever Wholly Lost*. New York: Simon & Schuster, 1995.

Parkes, Colin Murrary. *Bereavement: Studies of Grief in Adult Life*. 2nd ed. Madison, Conn.: International Universities Press, 1987.

Rando, Therese A. *How to Go on Living When Someone You Love Dies*. New York: Bantam, 1991.

Rapoport, Nessa. *A Woman's Book of Grieving*. New York: Morrow, 1994.

Sexton, Linda Gray. *Searching for Mercy Street: My Journey Back to My Mother, Anne Sexton*. Boston: Little, Brown, 1994.

Volkan, Vamik D., and Elizabeth Zintl. *Life after Loss: The Lessons of Grief.* New York: Scribner's, 1993.

Vozenilek, Helen, ed. *Loss of the Ground-Note: women writing about the loss of their mothers.* Los Angeles: Clothespin Fever Press, 1992.

Weenolsen, Patricia. *Transcendence of Loss over the Life Span.* New York: Hemisphere, 1988.

**Recommended Contemporary Novels About Mother Loss and Motherless Families:**

Davis, Thulani. *1959.* New York: HarperPerennial, 1992.

Gibbons, Kaye. *Ellen Foster.* New York: Vintage, 1987.

Godwin, Gail. *Father Melancholy's Daughter.* New York: Avon, 1991.

Minot, Susan. *Monkeys.* New York: Washington Square/Simon & Schuster, 1986.

Morris, Mary. *A Mother's Love.* New York: Talese-Doubleday, 1993.

Picoult, Jodi. *Harvesting the Heart.* New York: Viking, 1993.

Proulx, E. Annie. *The Shipping News.* New York: Touchstone/ Simon & Schuster, 1993.

Quindlen, Anna. *One True Thing.* New York: Random House, 1994.

Robinson, Marilynne. *Housekeeping*. New York: Bantam, 1982.

Smiley, Jane. *A Thousand Acres*. New York: Fawcett Columbine, 1992.

Tan, Amy. *The Joy Luck Club*. New York: Ivy Books, 1989.